Introduction to the

INTERNAL FAMILY SYSTEMS MODEL℠

Introduction to the

INTERNAL FAMILY SYSTEMS MODEL℠

RICHARD C. SCHWARTZ, PH.D.

Trailheads Publications

Oak Park, Illinois

ISBN: 978-0-9721480-0-9

Dedicated to

Regina "Reggie" Goulding
1954–2001

May her spirit continue to guide us.

Other books authored or coauthored by
Richard C. Schwartz

Internal Family Systems Therapy
Guilford Press

You Are the One You've Been Waiting For:
Bringing Courageous Love to Intimate Relationships
Trailheads Publications

Family Therapy: Concepts and Methods
Allyn and Bacon

The Mosaic Mind: Empowering the Tormented Selves
of Child Abuse Survivors
Trailheads Publications

Metaframeworks: Transcending the Models
of Family Therapy
Jossey-Bass

Handbook of Family Therapy
Training and Supervision
Guilford Press

Contents

Chapter One

THE INTERNAL FAMILY SYSTEMS MODEL

Have you ever heard someone say, "Before I can love someone else, I have to learn to love myself" or "My problem is that I lack self-esteem" or "I didn't want to do it, but I couldn't stop myself"? Who is the Self that we need to learn to love and esteem, and why is that so hard? Who is it that makes us do things we don't want to do? Will we be forever hounded by the critical voice in our head that calls us names all the time? Is there a better way to deal with the sense of worthlessness that sits in the pit of our stomach? How can we turn down the noise inside that keeps us anxious and distracted?

The Internal Family Systems (IFS) Model has a set of answers to questions like these that helps people begin to relate to themselves differently—to love themselves. It offers specific steps toward more control over impulsive or automatic reactions. It can transform your inner critical voice into a supportive one and can help you unload feelings of worthlessness. It is capable of helping you not only turn down the noise in your mind but also create an inner atmosphere of light and peace, bringing more confidence, clarity, and creativity to your relationships.

The IFS Model does this by first getting you to focus inside. By "focus inside," I mean to turn your attention toward your thoughts, emotions, fantasies, images, and sensations—your inner experience. This is a big step for most of us because we've been trained by our culture to keep our eyes fixed on the outside world, looking out there for danger as well as for satisfaction. That external focus makes sense because we have a lot to worry about and strive for in our environment, but there's another reason many of us don't enter our inner world—we're afraid of what's in there. We either know or suspect that deep within us lurk memories and feelings that could overwhelm us, making us feel horrible, impeding our ability to function, making us act impulsively, changing the way we relate to people, and making us vulnerable to being hurt again. This is particularly true if you were ever humiliated and made to feel worthless or if you have suffered losses or traumas in your life. To avoid revisiting any of that, you make sure you're always active or distracted, never giving the painful memories an opportunity to bubble up. You organize your life in ways that ensure nothing happens to trigger any of those dreaded memories or emotions. You strive to look and act acceptably, work hard to prove you're valuable, control how close or distant you get in relationships, take care of everyone so they'll like you, and so on.

Roger considers himself a competent professional, so he can't believe the way his mind goes blank every time his boss walks into his office. He can't stand the fact that her mere presence makes him feel so young and stupid. He has given himself pep talks before she comes in, has tried breathing exercises, and has criticized himself for being so fearful, but nothing works.

Susan is very invested in making sure her children like themselves, so she hates the way she sometimes "loses it" with her son. Every so often he'll do something small—leave his clothes lying around or come home late—and she finds herself yelling at him as if he'd just killed the cat. She often feels her strong reaction coming on, yet she just can't stop herself. Afterward she's wracked with guilt and hates herself for it, but it keeps happening.

Despite all he's accomplished, David is plagued by an underlying sense that he's worthless. People constantly praise him and tell him what a great person he is, but he can't take it in. He puts on a good front for others, but inside he's convinced that if they really knew him, they'd be disgusted. Intellectually, he knows he's well liked and he tries to convince himself of that, but the powerful feelings of worthlessness persist.

Kim can't control her eating. She's tried different diets, worked with nutritionists, and exercised like crazy, yet when the urge for sweets takes over, she's powerless. She detests the inner voice that seduces her into going to the refrigerator for pints of ice cream, but she can't resist its siren song.

Margot complains that she's only attracted to men who are bad for her. Plenty of nice guys are interested in her, but she only feels the chemistry with charismatic men who wind up treating her badly and rejecting her. She feels "doomed by [her] heart to a life of heartache."

What do all these people have in common? All of them were clients of mine who came to me because of an emotion or impulse they couldn't control. Not only that, but they fought with it constantly and were furious with themselves for not being able to control it. The uncontrollable impulse was bad enough, but the relationship they formed with it—their frustration with it and with themselves for having it—permeated their self-concept and made them feel worthless. I find this is often true. The way we relate to a troublesome thought or emotion not only doesn't succeed in controlling it but also compounds our problems. As Buddhist monk Thich Nhat Hanh puts it, "If we become angry at our anger, we will have two angers at the same time."

To better illustrate this idea, let's use an analogy to human relationships. Let's think of your anger as one of your children. Suppose you had a son whom you couldn't control—say he threw tantrums every night. That would be bad enough, but suppose that because those tantrums drove you crazy, you constantly criticized him and tried to keep him locked in his room for fear that he'd embarrass you in public. You stayed home on weekends to make sure he didn't run away and felt like a terrible parent because of his behavior. Suppose also that all of your reactions just made the tantrums worse because he sensed that you'd like to be rid of him. Because of the way you relate to your son, the problem comes to consume your life. The same is true with our extreme emotions and irrational beliefs—they're difficult enough, but the way we try to handle them often exacerbates them and makes our lives miserable.

It may seem strange to think of having a relationship with a thought or emotion, but we can't avoid it. They live with us, and we have to relate to them one way or another. Just as with difficult people in your family or work environment, how they affect you and how you interact with them will make a difference. Consider how you feel toward your various thoughts and emotions. Maybe you like the inner voice that reminds you of all the things you need to do and strategizes how to do them. You listen to it and use it as motivation; you relate to it as if it were a valued assistant. What about when you start to relax and that same voice becomes stridently critical, calling you lazy and telling you the sky will fall if you don't get back to work? How do you like it then? What do you say back to it? If you're like most people, you argue with it internally as if it were an oppressive boss. "Get off my back! Can't you let me sit still for even one minute? Lighten up!" Or you try to drown it out by watching TV or having a few drinks. The part of you that wants you to achieve makes for a wonderful servant but a terrible master, so you have a love/hate relationship with it.

We have ongoing, complex relationships with many different inner voices, thought patterns, and emotions that are similar to relationships we have with other people. What we call "thinking" is often our inner dialogues with different parts of us. Let's take another example. Think of someone you love who has died. How do you feel toward the grief you have about that person? Maybe you fear being overwhelmed by it and hate the way it brings you down. You try to keep it locked up somewhere in your psyche and avoid anything that might remind you of the dead loved one. You also get impatient with it: "Why do I still feel this way after all this time? I thought I'd already worked through all that." You try to turn it into an intrapsychic exile. Yet, like an exile, it keeps popping back up, overtaking you when you're not looking and throwing internal coups.

What about the part of you that gets extremely defensive when you argue with your intimate partner? In the middle of the fight, you suddenly become that part—seeing your partner through its eyes; taking on its distorted, black/white, blame/guilt perspective; stubbornly refusing to give an inch; and saying nasty things. Later you realize you were out of line and wonder, "Who was it that took over and behaved so obnoxiously? That wasn't me!" How do you feel toward that inner defender? If you're like most people, you don't like some aspects of it, but you feel so vulnerable during a fight that you rely on it for protection. You let it take over because you believe that without it your partner will blow you away. Your anger becomes like a tough bodyguard you like having around but wouldn't invite to dinner.

All the people I have described in this chapter came to me at war with themselves. They were knotted in dysfunctional inner relationships and, not surprisingly, their outer relationships paralleled their inner ones. By changing the way they regarded and interacted with their thoughts and emotions, they found that not only did the problem they brought to therapy improve dramatically, but, in general, they felt less inner turmoil, liked themselves more, and got along better with the people in their lives.

What was the direction of that change? They moved from hating, fearing, arguing with; trying to ignore, lock up, or get rid of; or giving in to and being overwhelmed by those feelings and beliefs—to becoming curious about them and listening to them. That initial curiosity often led to compassion for their emotions and thoughts, and attempts to help them.

I'll give an example from my own life. Whenever I had to give a presentation to an audience before I knew this new way of relating to myself, I'd become extremely anxious about how people would like it. As a child, I'd been humiliated in school, so a part of me is stuck in the past, each time certain I'll be humiliated again. The ironic thing about emotions like these is that they often create exactly the situation they fear. When the anxiety took over, I wouldn't be able to prepare well and would come across as insecure and inarticulate, so I got the very feedback that my anxiety feared I would. Because it had such a negative impact on my performance, I had good reason to consider the anxiety my enemy. Whenever I'd begin to feel it, I'd try to reassure myself, "Don't worry—you know what you're talking about, and no one wants you to look bad. Besides, even if you bomb, it's not going to be the end of your career." That kind of rational self-talk would work only briefly; then the anxiety would creep back in, so I'd get frustrated and escalate my self-criticism. "Why are you such a wimp?! Why can't you be like all those other people who do this with no sweat?" I'd have running inner conflicts like that up until the presentation. My talk generally would go fine, but I'd spend the next week picking apart every stupid thing I said or smart thing I forgot to say. The whole thing became a terrible ordeal that I dreaded.

Now I've learned a way of relating to my anxiety that makes such events interesting challenges rather than dreaded ordeals. Instead of attacking or ignoring my anxiety, I try to get into a curious state, focus inside on it, and ask it some questions. As I focus on the feeling, I notice that it seems to emanate from a knot in my gut, so I focus there while asking internally, "What are you so afraid of?" and then quietly await an answer. Within seconds I hear a weak "voice" (it's not really a voice as much as a thread of thoughts) spontaneously emerge from the murky depths of my mind and say, "I know I'll fail and be embarrassed again." Next, images from my past come to me—scenes of what happened in school long ago. Suddenly I'm filled with empathy and affection for that shy young kid who was shamed so severely and publicly for being unprepared. In my mind's eye, I hold that boy and remind him that I'm there and that he's not the one who has to do the presentation. I let him know that no matter what happens, I love him. He immediately calms down, and I sense the knot in my stomach release. That whole interaction takes less than a minute and I'm good to go, but that's because some years ago I spent several hours really getting to know that anxious part of me and changing my relationship with it. Now a quick reminder is all it needs.

It might sound strange to ask questions of an emotion, but have you ever felt angry or sad and not known why, and then after a day or so the answer just emerges from inside you? IFS offers a way to expedite that process, which helps you learn not only what your emotions are upset about but also how you can help them calm down and can find out what they need from you. It's a form of self-soothing that is easy for most people once they get the idea. The difficult part is to feel curiosity about or compassion for emotions or beliefs that you are used to hating and wanting to get rid of.

This may seem preposterous at first glance. Why would you want to focus on and try to feel compassion for the critical inner voice that makes you feel small, the paralyzing fear that freezes your brain in high-pressure situations, the anger that can suddenly hijack your mind and hurt others, and the sensitive part of you that's easily hurt and makes you feel worthless? It makes common sense not to go there and, instead, to try to lock all those thoughts and emotions out of your consciousness so you can avoid feeling bad and can function well. That's what we've been taught to do with difficult emotions and beliefs. But if that approach worked, you wouldn't be reading this book.

That approach is based on the misconception that our extreme emotions and beliefs are what they seem to be. If your anger, fear, self-hate, and sense of worthlessness are merely disturbed emotional states or learned irrational beliefs, it makes sense to try to use your "willpower" to lock them out, argue with them, or counter them with positive thoughts. It makes sense to form an authoritarian, coercive, or dismissive relationship with them because they seem like the enemy within. An unfortunate byproduct of that approach, however, is that you will form similar relationships with people around you who embody qualities of those enemies inside you. You'll become critical of or impatient with anyone who seems fearful, self-deprecating, ashamed, or aggressive.

In these pages, I hope to help you realize that your emotions and thoughts are much more than they seem—that those emotions and thoughts emanate from inner personalities I call *parts* of you. I'm suggesting that what seems like your explosive temper, for example, is more than a bundle of anger. If you were to focus on it and ask it questions, you might learn that it is a protective part of you that defends other vulnerable parts and is in conflict with the parts of you that want to please everyone. It might reveal to you that it has to stay this angry as long as you are so vulnerable and self-sacrificing. You might also learn that it has other feelings, such as fear and sadness, but that it feels as though it must stay in this role of being the angry one to protect you. If you asked it to, it could show you scenes of the point in your life when it was forced into its protective role. It might even show you an image or representation of itself, such as a dragon, volcano, or tough adolescent kid. Most importantly, it can tell you how you can help to release it so it is no longer stuck in this rageful role. With your help, it can change dramatically into a valuable quality so that you're no longer plagued with a bad temper and instead, for example, have an increased ability to assert yourself appropriately.

That last paragraph may have triggered a part of you that's saying, "This sounds really weird. He's saying I have all these little people inside me who can talk back to me. What does he think, that I'm Sybil?" I don't blame you for being skeptical. I was, too, when my clients initially began talking to me about their parts, but it's one of those things that's difficult to accept until you've experienced it. Until you focus inside, begin intentional conversations with your emotions and thoughts, and are surprised by the answers that come, this will be very hard to believe. I'm not asking you to take it from me—I'm simply inviting you to keep your mind open to this possibility and do your own exploring. Find out for yourself if what I'm saying is possible—that you can help your inner antagonists become your allies. Perhaps this is what Jesus meant when he said, "Love your enemies."

It is this understanding of our disturbing thoughts and emotions—that they are manifestations of inner personalities that have been forced into extreme roles by events in our lives—which leads us to relate to them differently. It's easy to have compassion for an inner teenager who tried valiantly to protect you in the past and who ended up frozen in time in that angry role, or for a little boy who is terrified to be humiliated again. With this understanding, we begin to reverse the dysfunctional internal relationships we have formed with many different parts of us and that our parts have formed with one another. As our parts feel more accepted and less threatened or attacked, they transform; once we kiss them, our frogs become princes. As a bonus, we find ourselves more accepting of, and less reactive to, people who used to bother us. We can relate to them with compassion because we're able to do that with the parts of us that resemble them. Sometimes we find that those people transform, too—or at least that our perception of and relationship with them transforms.

Think of how your work environment would be altered if the leaders in your organization related to themselves differently. If they hate the parts of themselves that want to slow down and enjoy life, they will be impatient with workers who aren't as driven as they are. If they want to get rid of their own insecurity and anxiety, they'll create an atmosphere in which people fear for their jobs if they show vulnerability. If they attack themselves for making mistakes, everyone will pretend to be perfect. If they fear their own inner critics, they'll fear the judgment of others and let people become exploitive. On the other hand, if they can relate to those parts of themselves in caring ways, that compassion and acceptance will permeate the company, making it much easier for all the employees to relate compassionately to their own parts and to one another. The same process applies to your inner family.

This new way of relating to yourself can't be forced. It doesn't work to command yourself to be curious about these parts of you or pretend to feel compassion for them. It has to be genuine. So how do you get to that point? This raises the question of who the "you" is who relates to your parts. Who are you at your core?

The most wonderful discovery I have made is that as you do this work, you release, or liberate, what I'll call your Self or your True Self. I find that as people focus on—and, in the process of doing that, separate from—their extreme emotions and thoughts, they spontaneously manifest qualities that make for good leadership, both internally and externally. It seems that we all have qualities like curiosity, compassion, calmness, confidence, courage, clarity, creativity, and connectedness at our core. It's the soul that spiritual traditions talk about but that most psychotherapies don't know about. Your Self gets obscured by all the fear, anger, and shame—all the extreme emotions and beliefs that are pumped into you during your life—so you may not even know it's there.

If you're like most people, you have only caught glimpses of your Self. Maybe your constant inner conversation with and among your parts stopped suddenly when you "lost yourself" in a creative or athletic activity, in the beauty of a sunset or the innocence of children at play, or in a dangerous activity like rock climbing that requires total present-centered awareness. You might remember those experiences as brief moments of complete joy and deep peace. Perhaps you had a fleeting experience of connection to something bigger than yourself and the sense of well-being that accompanies that awareness. You may have dismissed those episodes as anomalies in your otherwise roiling and noisy stream of consciousness and may have assumed you are the noise rather than the peace that lies beneath it. But what if that peaceful, joyful, connected state is who you really are? How might that change your self-concept? And, what if, in addition to having brief peaceful and joyful moments, it were possible to be in that state for long periods of time while going about your daily activities or even while you're in a conflict with someone? Finally, what if, while in that Self state, you not only felt good, but you spontaneously manifested qualities like guileless curiosity, open-hearted compassion, clarity of perception, and intuitive wisdom about how to relate harmoniously to your parts and to the people in your life? If all that were true, your life could be very different. I have good news for you: all of that is true.

This book is based on an approach to psychotherapy called the Internal Family Systems (IFS) Model, so named because it's as if we each have a family of parts living within us. An IFS therapist first helps a client to focus on and get to know the parts that protect him or her. Then the client asks those parts to relax, to separate their feelings and beliefs from the client in order to open more space inside. As this happens, clients spontaneously report feeling calm, curious, and compassionate—the qualities of Self—toward their parts. I don't have to ask a client to try to feel that way; those qualities just naturally emerge, as if released, when parts relax and separate.

For example, Ted is afraid of his inner critic. As long as he can remember, he has felt oppressed by its constant judgment. When he focuses on it, he finds it in his head and says he hates it. I ask him to change his focus to the part that hates the critic and ask it to separate itself from him. That angry part agrees to do so. I ask Ted how he feels toward the critic now. In a calmer, more confident voice, he says, "I wonder why it feels the need to do this to me." He says his image of it has changed, too. At first it looked like a giant, menacing figure of his father, but now it has shrunk considerably and looks quite a bit younger. No longer intimidated by his critic, Ted begins listening to it tell him about how hard it works to get him to perform perfectly so that no one will criticize him. Also, it believes that if it makes him feel terrible, he'll be prepared for negative judgments from other people. As he listens, Ted feels increasing gratitude for its attempts to protect him, as well as empathy for how much fear of rejection he senses that it carries. When Ted tells the part he feels that way, the former cold-blooded tormentor breaks down and weeps while Ted holds it. As poet Rainer Maria Rilke wrote, "Perhaps all the dragons of our lives are princesses who are only waiting to see us once beautiful and brave. Perhaps everything terrible is in its deepest being something helpless that wants help from us."

Once released from his fear, Ted knew what to do to help his critic. Very little leading was needed from me after his anger separated; Ted took over and seemed to know just how to help it. That is a common occurrence in IFS therapy. Just as our bodies know how to heal physical injuries, it seems that we all possess an innate wisdom for healing ourselves emotionally. The difficulty is in accessing that wisdom. IFS provides clear, practical ways to do that and helps you bring more Self into your life in general. It offers a new, uplifting self-concept, a clear and effective way of understanding and working with your troublesome emotions and thoughts, and a method for bringing more Self-leadership into your daily life so you spend more time in, and relate to others from, a state of deep peace and joy. The first step toward those goals is to help you become aware that you are much more than you have been taught.

EXERCISES

Becoming aware of inner family relationships

Take a few moments to think about the relationships you have formed with your different thoughts, emotions, or inner voices. The following is a list of parts that most people experience and sometimes feel oppressed by. After you read each one, consider how you relate to it—how you feel toward it, what you do or say inside when you experience it, how successfully you've exiled it from your life, and how much your relationship with it affects your life.

sexual thoughts or urges

*the inner voice that criticizes your appearance
or performance*

*anxiety that freezes your mind
in high-performance situations*

the urge to eat or drink too much

jealous or possessive feelings about your partner

yearning for intimacy

*worries that flash worst-case scenarios
in your mind about the future*

grief about someone who has died or left you

a nagging sense of worthlessness

*the voice that tells you that you're not working
hard enough and won't let you relax*

*fear that keeps you from taking social risks
and inhibits your liveliness*

the urge to care for everyone and neglect yourself

*the anger that surges forth
when you feel hurt by someone*

sensitive feelings that can be easily hurt

*loneliness that comes up when you're
not distracted or with people*

*competitiveness that makes you feel bad when you learn
that others are doing better than you*

the need to be in control of everything or everyone

an underlying sense of incompetence

the happy or "together" mask you hide behind

*the perfectionist inside you that can't allow
any mistakes or blemishes*

judgmental thoughts you have about other people

*the inertia that makes you sit in front of the TV
or lie in bed*

*a sense of hopelessness that makes small tasks
seem overwhelming*

dissatisfaction with your place in life or your achievements

the belief that you have been victimized in life

I expect you found at least a few thoughts or emotions on the list that you have trouble accepting and instead wish you were rid of. Maybe you have gotten rid of some of them to the extent that you don't experience them very often and don't think of yourself as that kind of person. Pick one item from the list that you had a strong reaction to and think about how hard it would be to change the way you relate to it. Can you imagine approaching it with curiosity and trying to listen to it rather than scolding it or shooing it away? Curiosity is often the first step because until you have heard its reasons for being the way it is, you'll have trouble feeling compassion for it. What fears come to mind as you contemplate this kind of change in your inner relationships?

. . . .

Contemplating who you really are

What are your fundamental beliefs about human nature? Are we, at our essence, selfish and aggressive, or have you had personal experiences that contradict this view? How might your view of yourself change if you accepted the idea that your core Self is inherently good, wise, courageous, compassionate, joyful, and calm? Take a few minutes to imagine how your life would be different if you had more access to those qualities on a daily basis and trusted that this calm, joyful Self was your true identity. Think about what might change in relationships with key people in your personal life, in your work or school life, and in future choices you might make.

Contemplating your multiplicity

Try on, for a second, the idea that your thoughts and emotions emanate from discrete personalities inside you. What fears arise as you consider that possibility? People often have fears that come from the association to conditions like schizophrenia or multiple personality disorder (now called dissociative identity disorder), or from the creepy idea that autonomous entities exist within us—that we are not fully in control of ourselves. If you can put aside those fears for a second, consider what might be good about having parts. What would it be like if you knew with confidence that your most repulsive or disdainful thoughts or feelings were coming from little parts of you rather than being the essence of your identity? How would it feel to disclose shameful feelings to others if you could say "Part of me feels . . ." rather than "I feel . . ."? What if you totally trusted that those parts were different from your true Self and that you, as that Self, could help them to transform?

Chapter Two

THE SELF

For you to move in the direction of releasing your Self, you first have to know it is there. If you don't have any idea of who you really are, you can't become that person. You will disregard any fleeting experiences of Self as aberrations or illusions and will adhere to the limiting self-concepts you've been taught. When asked how he created the magnificent David from a block of marble, Michelangelo is reputed to have said, "I knew he was in there and just needed someone to let him out." If you know you have a magnificent essence that's encrusted in calcified emotions and beliefs, you can set to work on releasing that essence. If you don't know it exists, you resign yourself to experiencing life through a protective covering.

In this chapter, we will explore this idea of the Self because it is the centerpiece of the IFS Model and is the hardest piece for most people to fully accept. The idea that at your essence you are pure joy and peace, and that from that place you are able to manifest clusters of wonderful leadership and healing qualities and sense a spiritual connectedness, runs counter to what you've learned about yourself. A variety of beliefs run through our culture regarding human nature, and none of them is terribly uplifting. The most obvious of these is the doctrine of Original Sin, started by St. Augustine and promoted by much of Western Christianity since his time. According to this notion, because of the Fall— Adam and Eve's transgression—humanity has been cursed to be born in sin and to have a base, selfish constitution. According to that perspective, our passions are evidence of our ongoing sinful state. We must spend our lives controlling passionate emotions and impulses, and reminding ourselves of our basic sinfulness. While many contemporary Christians have moved away from that position, it has had a huge impact on Western culture's beliefs about people. Those beliefs didn't exist in Christianity before St. Augustine and, in fact, many early Christian leaders subscribed to the opposite belief, which might be called "Original Blessing."

Another hugely influential position draws from Charles Darwin's theory of evolution. Darwin's view of human nature corresponds closely to Original Sin, but with a scientific cast. He posited that our selfish nature is the product of our genes, which program us to fight for survival in a competitive, hostile environment. We can see these cultural myths of the Fall and the "selfish gene" reflected in some of our most influential psychologies. For example, Freudian, behavioral, and evolutionary psychologies teach that everything we do is designed to maximize pleasure or to expand our gene pool. This view of ourselves as fundamentally selfish or sinful leads to harsh, punitive methods for controlling our parts and other people.

Then there's developmental psychology, which maintains that our basic nature is dependent on the kind of parenting we received. If you were fortunate to have "good enough" parenting during certain critical periods in your early development, you emerged from childhood with a certain amount of "ego strength." If you didn't, you were out of luck. You remain defective and pathological until you have some type of corrective reparenting experience from a therapist or significant other. This perspective—that if we have any valuable qualities, they had to have been pumped into us from the outside world—is another prevalent and influential one. It's the basis of the theories of learning that dominate our educational system. We think we must be taught morality, empathy, and respect because those values are not inherent in us. This philosophy teaches us to look outside ourselves to get our needs met, and it encourages therapists to try to give their clients what they believe the clients lack rather than help them find those qualities within themselves. These views of ourselves as environmentally dependent, bereft, and ignorant lead us to search for the right "expert" to solve our problems and lead helpers to take on a pedagogical or parental role. We are discouraged from taking a leadership role with our parts and in our lives.

Journey to the Self

It may help you entertain the possibility that what you've learned about yourself is wrong if I briefly describe my own journey to that conclusion. When I first began to work as a therapist in the late 1970s, I held the view that I had to give my clients crucial insights and suggestions. The fact that they had problems indicated to me that they were lacking something and were paying me to provide it for them. I also had absorbed from the culture a cynical picture of people—and of myself—as basically self-serving and fear-driven, and, from my clinical training, the view that people were bundles of pathology. I wasn't open to the possibility of the Self, although I had had glimpses. Like many other young people in the sixties, I had experimented with meditation to find respite from my inner cacophony. While focused on my mantra, my mind quieted down and I sensed other dimensions of myself, but I had no framework for understanding them. Also, I was an athlete who, on the football field and basketball court, had occasionally entered that delicious flow state in which my mind was still and my body could do no wrong. Like most people, however, I was mostly consumed with finding ways to counter the undercurrent of worthlessness that ran through my psyche. I believed the inner voices that told me I was basically lazy, stupid, and selfish. That's who I thought I really was.

I was led to knowledge about the Self later in my therapy career through witnessing what happened to my clients as I helped them explore their inner worlds. At that time, in the early 1980s, I was a zealous family therapist who believed family therapy had found the holy grail by using systems thinking to understand and change family structures. Like most family therapists at that time, I had little interest in my own or my clients' intrapsychic lives. I thought there was no need to look inside people when all you needed to do to solve their problems was get them to change their relationships with other family members. My clients, however, didn't cooperate. I suffered what Aldous Huxley called "a slaying of a beautiful hypothesis by an ugly fact." That fact was that no matter how well family relationships were reorganized, people's inner lives still had tremendous power over them.

Out of that frustration, I began asking clients what kinds of thoughts and feelings were keeping them stuck in old ruts. I had several clients at that time who began talking about different parts of them as if those "parts" were autonomous voices or subpersonalities. For example, a lovely young woman I'll call Diane spoke of her pessimist voice and her critic, which accompanied her every positive action with their songs of doom and gloom. She said she had other voices that argued with these predictors of failure and still others that would just feel ashamed and incompetent. She considered the shame and incompetence to be the "real Diane." As a family therapist, I was intrigued by these inner battles. I began asking Diane and other clients to try to alter them in the same ways in which I'd been trying to change conflicts in families. In other words, as described earlier, I began to focus on Diane's relationship with her thoughts and emotions.

It seemed that Diane and many other clients could actually converse with these thoughts and feelings as if they were real personalities. I had Diane ask her pessimist voice why it always told her she was hopeless. To my amazement, she said that it answered her. It told her she was hopeless to keep her from taking risks and getting hurt—in other words, it was trying to protect her. This seemed like a promising interaction. If this pessimist really had benign intent, Diane might be able to negotiate a different role for it. Yet Diane wasn't interested. She was angry at this voice and told it to just leave her alone. When I asked her why she was being rude to the pessimist, she went on a long diatribe, describing how that voice had turned every step in her life into a major hurdle. It then occurred to me that I was not talking to Diane but rather to a different part of her that constantly fought with the pessimist. In an earlier conversation, Diane had told me about an ongoing war inside her between a voice that pushed her to achieve and the pessimist, which told her that her efforts were hopeless. It seemed that the pushing part had jumped in while she was talking to the pessimist.

I asked Diane to focus on the voice that was so angry at the pessimist and ask it to stop interfering in her negotiations with it. Again to my amazement, it agreed to "step back," and Diane immediately shifted out of the anger she had felt so strongly just seconds before. When I asked Diane how she felt toward the pessimist now, it seemed as though a different person answered. In a calm, caring voice, she said she was grateful to it for trying to protect her and felt sorry that it had to work so hard. Her face and posture had also changed, reflecting the soft compassion in her voice. From that point on, negotiations with the pessimist were easy.

I tried this "step back" procedure with several other clients. Sometimes we had to ask two or three voices not to interfere before a client shifted into a state similar to Diane's, but we got there nonetheless. I began to get excited. What if people could get extreme voices to step back simply by asking them to, not only in negotiations with other parts but also with family members, bosses, anyone? What if the person who was left when the parts stepped back was always as compassionate as Diane and these other clients had become?

When they were in that calm, compassionate state, I asked these clients what voice or part was there. They each gave a variation of the following reply: "That's not a part like those other voices are. That's more of who I really am—that's my Self." Without knowing it, I had stumbled onto a new way of helping people access the Self that so many spiritual traditions described, but I didn't realize this until years later. At the time, I was simply thrilled to have found a way to make therapy so much more effortless and effective for my clients as well as for me.

This serendipitous discovery in the early 1980s—that as I helped clients separate from their extreme emotions and beliefs, they would immediately and spontaneously shift into their Self— was confusing as well as thrilling. In several cases, they would suddenly demonstrate a kind of ego strength I never suspected they had. Some of these clients not only hadn't had good enough parenting when they were very young, but also had been tortured and deprecated on a daily basis. Some had never been held or comforted in their lives. Their childhoods had been nightmares of fear and degradation. So where could they have gotten these qualities that were springing forth? There was no way they could have absorbed these qualities from the abusive people on whom they had depended when they were children.

I began questioning the assumptions of developmental psychology and learning theory. I wondered, *Is it possible that we are born with such qualities and don't need to obtain them from our environments? How could it be that our psychologies, philosophies, and religions have so thoroughly underestimated human nature?* It was only after several years of testing this possibility with scores of clients—and finding over and over that once their parts separated, they spontaneously embodied qualities of the Self—that I released my ingrained cynicism and fully embraced the exciting conviction that there was much more to us than we had previously thought.

Since I could find so little in Western psychology to confirm these optimistic observations, I began looking elsewhere. I learned that the kind of Self I encountered in my clients was described by various spiritual traditions around the world.

The secret of the gods

According to an ancient legend, there was a time when the gods were trying to decide where to hide the secret to peace and joy. They didn't want humans to find it until they were ready to appreciate it. One god said, "Let's hide it on the highest mountain." Another said, "No, it would be found there too soon and too easily." Another god suggested hiding it deep in the densest forest, but that location was rejected for the same reason. After many other suggestions and rejections, the wisest god said, "Hide it in the human heart—that's the last place they'll look." The gods all agreed, so that's where they put it.

The gods were very wise. The last place we look for peace and joy is inside ourselves. We search everywhere else: in intimate relationships, careers, purchases, travel, gurus, self-help groups, and the grace of God above. Yet over the centuries in different parts of the world, small groups of people have looked inside and have found the secret that the gods hid. They are known as the esoteric or mystical branches of all the world's religions. (As used here, the term *esoteric* does not refer to something exotic or "far out." Instead it comes from the Greek *esotero,* which means "further in." Esoteric traditions are those that have looked further inside people, in contrast to conventional, exoteric religions.) Though they use different words, all these groups say the same thing: we are sparks of the eternal flame, drops of the divine ocean, manifestations of the absolute ground of being. But because we don't look inside, we have little awareness of who we really are. Once we learn to hold awareness of who we really are, we find peace and joy.

As I explored the writings of some of these esoteric schools, it gradually dawned on me that through interacting with people's parts in ways that allowed the individuals to separate from their emotions and beliefs, I had accidentally come upon a simple way to help people access the state of consciousness that those traditions sought through meditation and other techniques. I had stumbled onto the secret of the gods.

Who's there when you step back?

Actually, the process of focusing on a part of you and asking it to "step back" is similar to forms of meditation in which people separate from and witness their thoughts. For example, a popular form of Buddhist meditation called *vipassana* involves simply witnessing each thought or emotional state that arises. The more you notice—step back from—rather than become or identify with your thoughts and emotions, the more you relax into being the "you" who is not your thoughts and emotions. Many traditions speak of this as being a "state of emptiness," of "no-self." What they often mean is no ego or conditioned mind, what I call "no parts."

Knowledge of this special place within us is not limited to Eastern traditions. Thomas Merton, one of the most significant Christian scholars and writers of the twentieth century, wrote:

> If we enter into ourselves, finding our true self, and then passing "beyond" the inner "I," we sail forth into the immense darkness in which we confront the "I am" of the Almighty. . . . Our inmost "I" exists in God and God swells in it. . . . Hence the Christian mystical experience is not only an awareness of the inner self, but also . . . it is an experiential grasp of God as present within our inner self. (quoted in Pennington, 1993, p. 119)

Merton developed a meditative practice called *centering prayer* that has become widespread among Christians in the West due in large part to the efforts of Father Thomas Keating, who agrees that "God and our true Self are not separate" (1997, p. 127). The Quakers call it the *Inner Light*. The Buddhists call it *rigpa*, or *Buddha Nature*. Hindus call it *Atman* or the *Self*. Meister Eckhart called it the *Godseed*. For Sufis, it's the *Beloved*—the God within.

Whether you believe it is God inside you or simply a higher level of consciousness, there is consensus among traditions around the world that such a place exists within us and that it is not difficult to tap into. The words used by different traditions to describe the Self state—*inherent wisdom and compassion, a sense of freedom, lightness, release, stability, lucidity*—are some of the qualities my clients report and display when their parts step back and their Self is released. People have known for centuries about this peaceful state that I am calling the *Self*. The more I explored this spiritual territory, the more I felt the way Ralph Waldo Emerson did when he said, "All my best ideas were stolen by the ancients."

But that state is not the exclusive domain of spiritual explorers. Other nonspiritual practitioners have also recognized the benefits derived from turning down the mind's noise. For example, Betty Edwards, author of *Drawing on the Right Side of the Brain*, found that people can draw much better than they believed possible when in that state. Tim Gallwey, who wrote *The Inner Game of Tennis*, sparked a wide variety of books that describe how much better athletes perform when in this state. The developer of biofeedback, Elmer Green, found that when people achieved the theta brain wave state—a place of deep relaxation, full of imagery—they could produce remarkable control over physiological processes that were considered uncontrollable. That discovery led Eugene Peniston to train chronic alcoholics to achieve theta. The finding that they quit drinking opened the field of biofeedback training to treat a wide range of disorders. This state has been called "flow" by researcher Mihalyi Csikszentmihalyi, who found that it characterized the experience of all kinds of creative and high-performing people.

Thus it seems clear that this mindful state of Self is not just a peaceful place from which to witness the world nor just a state to which one can go to transcend the world; the Self also has healing, creative, and performance-enhancing qualities. When my clients entered this Self state, they didn't just passively witness their parts—they began to actively interact with them in creative and healing ways. Diane and the others began relating to their parts in ways that the parts seemed to need. These clients began to bring forth their emergent compassion, lucidity, and wisdom to get to know and care for these inner personalities. Some parts, such as Diane's pessimist, needed to hear from her that, while at one time in her life she had been very hurt and had to withdraw, it no longer needed to protect her in that way. Subpersonalities such as the pessimist seemed like inner trauma victims, stuck in the past, their minds frozen around a time of great distress. Others needed to be held, comforted, loved, or just listened to. We are so used to fighting and wanting to be rid of parts like these that we have no idea who they really are.

The most amazing thing of all was that once in that Self state, clients seemed to know just what to do or say to help each inner personality. It gradually became clear that I didn't have to teach them how to relate differently to these thoughts and emotions they were calling parts; either they would automatically begin doing what the part needed, or they would begin asking questions that would lead to ways of helping the part. My job was mainly to try to help clients remain in the state of Self and then get out of their way as they became therapists to their own inner families.

The Self-Led Person

I was also finding that when clients accessed their Self, they began relating differently to the people around them in addition to parts within them. It seemed that before they began doing IFS work, most clients had parts that didn't trust the leadership of their Self in the outside world. These parts jumped in to handle many kinds of external experiences because they believed they had to protect the system. They were like parentified children who don't trust that their parent is capable and, consequently, bravely take on responsibilities for the welfare of the family that are beyond their capacities.

As this changed—as these protective parts began to trust the clients' Self to lead more in the outside world—either my clients' relationships became more harmonious or they found the courage to leave relationships that had been exploitive. They became less reactive in crises and less overwhelmed by emotional episodes that used to do them in. During such episodes, they would report that they now understood that a *part* of them, not *all* of them, was upset, so rather than blending with the part, they would notice it and then try to comfort it. They didn't always succeed in calming it down, but just the awareness that they were not the part helped them remain more centered. They could wait until the storm blew over, secure in the knowledge that their Self would reemerge—that the sun would shine again.

After you get to know your own Self, you can sense when some degree of Self is present in people around you and when it's not. A person who is leading with the Self is easy to identify. To rephrase a joke, you get the impression that "the lights are on and someone is home." Others describe such a person as open, confident, and accepting—as having presence. You feel immediately at ease in a Self-led person's company, sensing that it is safe to relax and release your own Self. Such a person often generates remarks like, "I like him because I don't have to pretend—I can be myself with him." From the person's eyes, voice, body language, and energy, you can tell you are in the presence of someone who is authentic, solid, and unpretentious. You are attracted by the Self-led person's lack of agenda or need for self-promotion, as well as by his or her passion for life and commitment to service. Such a person doesn't need to be forced by moral or legal rules to do the right thing. He or she is naturally compassionate and motivated to improve the human condition in some way because of the awareness that we are all connected.

Whenever I begin describing the qualities of a Self-led person, it triggers parts of me that feel inadequate. While at times I can embody some of those qualities, more often I'm a far cry from that person. I believe one of the mistakes that some organized religions make is in holding up the image of a saintly person as a model of what their followers should be, yet providing little practical advice on getting there other than by using willpower or prayer. As a result, people feel chronically inferior and become angry at their emotions and thoughts that aren't so evolved.

To avoid that pitfall, it's important to remember that very few people are constantly and fully Self-led. On the rocky road of life, we are all, to varying degrees, rejected, humiliated, abandoned, and traumatized. We all have pools of pain and shame, and protective strategies that are reinforced by our culture. We all come to distrust our Self and put on a range of masks. Until those pools are fully drained and our protectors fully relax, Self-leadership will be fleeting at best. We move into Self-leadership by degrees, slowly accruing moments of inner and outer flow, gradually finding that we are not obliterated when we keep our heart open in the face of anger or that the sky doesn't fall when we pause our constant worrying, and finding that we can comfort hurting inner children rather than being overwhelmed by them or exiling them. Margery Williams Bianco (1999), in the children's book *The Velveteen Rabbit,* helps us with the long-term perspective:

"What is REAL?" asked the Rabbit one day . . . "Does it happen all at once, or bit by bit?"

"It doesn't happen all at once," said the Skin Horse. "You become. It takes a long time. That's why it doesn't often happen to people who break easily, or have sharp edges, or who have to be carefully kept. Generally, by the time you are REAL, most of your hair has been loved off, and your eyes drop out and you get loose in the joints and very shabby. But these things don't matter at all, because once you are REAL you can't be ugly, except to people who don't understand."

The IFS Model presents a path toward becoming more real—toward increased Self-leadership. It helps you learn how to break less easily, soften your sharp edges, and not have to manage yourself so carefully. It is not always an easy or quick path, but most people begin feeling much better long before their hair is loved off and their eyes drop out. It's also true that once Self-led, your appearance matters much less and you know that you can't be ugly.

Few people come to me asking for increased Self-leadership, however. They come because they feel oppressed by people or situations, or by their emotions, thoughts, or symptoms. As they access their Self to untangle the knotted inner relationships related to those oppressions, they find that not only do the problems they entered therapy for improve, but, as a bonus, their overall outlook and functioning do as well. They have more Self in their lives.

Qualities of the Self

Let's continue to examine the qualities of the Self. As we've discussed, there is agreement among the world's esoteric traditions that such a state exists in us. In most of those traditions, however, messages suggest that language is inadequate to capture this concept of Self. That may be so, but because different people describe similar experiences and display similar qualities when in that state, we can describe aspects of those experiences and qualities. To clarify this discussion, I find it useful to differentiate between what people report while meditating—while being reabsorbed into the ocean—and what people are like when their Self is actively leading their everyday life—while being a separate wave of the ocean.

It is that oceanic state which seems so difficult to describe. People report feeling as if they have no boundaries, are one with the universe, and lose their identity as a separate being. This is accompanied by a sense of spaciousness in body and mind that can provide an experience of great contentment as well as moments of bliss. People often feel a pulsating energy or warmth running through their body and may sense light in or around them. As they deepen their meditative practice, people encounter different levels and stages, which the different esoteric traditions have explored and charted. Ken Wilber's work provides a good summary of those ascending stages of consciousness. My purpose here is less to acquaint you with those ethereal realms than to help you bring some of that awareness, spaciousness, and energy to your daily tasks and relationships. What qualities do people report and display when they live in the world while holding the memory of who they really are? What are the characteristics of Self-leadership?

I don't know the full answer to that question. After twenty years of helping people move toward greater Self-leadership, I can describe what my clients exhibit as they increasingly embody Self. As I sifted through various adjectives to capture my observations, I repeatedly came up with words that begin with the letter C, so now we will travel the eight Cs of Self-leadership.

Calmness

A pervasive sense of physiological and mental calm accompanies Self-leadership. Many people, especially those who have experienced traumas, feel constant tension in their body, as if they contain a tightly wound spring, which makes them hypervigilant and agitated. If you're like them, this state of physical arousal makes you overreact to other people and prevents you from ever truly relaxing. Your mind reflects this aroused state, with thoughts and urges jumping around, to use the Buddhist metaphor, like a hyperactive or drunken monkey.

As you embody your Self, you will be relieved to find far less activity in your body and mind. As a result, you will react to triggers in your environment in less automatic and extreme ways. The monkeys in your mind become mellow, basking in the reduction in worries and responsibilities that comes with trusting your Self to handle the world. In the face of anger, you aren't overwhelmed by the common fight, flight, or freeze impulses and instead maintain an inner equanimity. Many people appear to be calm on the outside but internally are a frenzy of activity. Many of us have been trained to hide our distress behind a calm, thoughtful exterior, but that is being frozen, not calm.

This is not to say that Self-led people walk around in a Buddha-like state of serene detachment. They ride on the roller coaster of life like everyone else. It's just that, for them, the ride that used to produce a white-knuckled clinging more often becomes interesting and sometimes painful or joyful. Where they used to be totally absorbed by each emotion or totally cut off from each one, they now experience the waves of feeling but also hold a calm center that is never totally washed away—the center of the cyclone, what I call the *"I" in the storm*.

Clarity

I define clarity as the ability to perceive situations without distortion from extreme beliefs and emotions—in other words, seeing through the eyes of the Self. As someone who has worked extensively with eating-disordered clients, I have seen how powerfully parts of us can affect our perceptions. When a rail-thin anorexic client looks in the mirror, she literally sees a fat person. But that is only an extreme example of the kind of distorting we do all the time. For example, recall a time when you were infatuated with someone. Perhaps you became oblivious to conspicuous red flags. Then, when that same person did something hurtful, it's likely that all you could see were the person's flaws, and you wondered what you used to like about him or her. A traditional story illustrates this point well:

> A man whose axe was missing suspected his neighbor's son. The boy walked like a thief, looked like a thief, and spoke like a thief. Soon the man found his axe while he was digging in the valley, and the next time he saw his neighbor's son, the boy walked, looked, and spoke like any other child.

In other words, we rarely take a fresh, open look at a person or situation because we so quickly and automatically jump to conclusions based on previous experience and current desire. As the expression goes, "To a man with a hammer, everything looks like a nail." I had a client, Bill, for example, who was desperate to get married. A part of him immediately rated every woman he met as a potential mate or not. In addition, Bill felt he had been rejected by his mother at an early age, so a protective part sized up every potential mate as like Mom (that is, dangerous) or not. To complicate things, Bill had always hoped to be accepted by his mother, so another part of him wanted the potential mate to be like Mom and would not let him feel attracted to women who were not. Every woman he met unwittingly stepped into his radar system with all its conflicting categories, and her qualities were distorted or ignored accordingly. The women he dated complained about getting many mixed messages and stated that he didn't really know them. They were right.

For Bill to really know any of these women, he would need to get all these parts and their projections to step back and let his Self experience the women. When that is possible, we have what the Buddhists call "beginner's mind," a perspective in which many possibilities exist because of the absence of preconception and projection. In contrast, the expert's mind is overflowing with beliefs that limit perception and possibility. Our parts often think they are experts on the world. The Self always has a beginner's mind.

Curiosity

In addition to containing many possibilities, the beginner's mind is also full of wonder about the world. If we don't prejudge things, we are perpetually curious. Like an inquisitive child, we are full of innocent interest in people and their reactions. If people are angry at us and our view of them isn't clouded by feelings connected with others who have been angry at us in the past, we become curious about their anger. When we ask them about it, they will sense no fear or judgment in our question—just innocent interest.

This kind of curiosity is at the heart of the IFS approach. It is how the Self relates not only to people but also to inner voices. When we are able to become nonjudgmentally interested in even our most despised inner demons (such as contempt, racism, and self-hate), we find those internal dialogues to be enlightening and transformative. The Buddhists call this kind of nonstriving, open curiosity toward our inner thoughts and emotions *mindfulness*. Many of their practices are designed to help people become more mindful.

That kind of pure, guileless curiosity is disarming. People and parts of us sense that they no longer must protect themselves because they see that we intend only to try to understand them. Since all they usually want is to be understood, they have no reason to remain angry or defensive. Instead, they are often glad to tell their story and feel heard by a person who is not trying to change them. In this book, this is what is meant by the term *witnessing*—asking about and listening to a person or part with genuine curiosity and with the intent to achieve the next quality: compassion.

Compassion

When your view of people is not distorted by the parts of you that fear or need them, you are not as affected by the ways they protect themselves. Then your curiosity can lead you to see behind their anger or distancing and learn about the hurt they are protecting.

To clarify what is meant by compassion, I want to contrast it to pity and to empathy. With pity, you see someone suffering and you feel sorry for him or her, but at the same time a part of you is glad that person isn't you. Your mind is busy thinking of reasons you wouldn't make the mistakes he or she made that led to the suffering. Pity involves both a protective distancing and a measure of condescension. Your sorrow for the sufferer comes from a place of separateness.

When you feel empathy, you see a person suffering, and

because you have a certain level of self-awareness, you know a part of you suffers in the same way, so you identify with the sufferer's pain. At some level, that person is the same as you. Empathy opens your heart and produces a strong desire to help the person. The danger with empathy, however, is that if you identify too much, you will feel a pressure to relieve the other's misery. You can't tolerate your own pain, so you can't stand for the other to spend any time suffering. The other common consequence of having too much empathy is to distance from the other person because his or her pain makes you hurt too much.

When you feel compassion, you see a person suffering, you feel empathy for him or her, and you know that the other has a Self which, once released, can relieve his or her own misery. If people relieve their own suffering, they learn to trust their own Self, and they learn whatever lessons the suffering has to teach them. Compassion, then, leads to doing whatever possible to foster the release of the other's Self rather than become the other's healer. With compassion, you can be open-heartedly present with sufferers without feeling the urge to change them or distance from them. This kind of Self-presence will often release their own Self. (There are, of course, situations in which the other's Self cannot be released while he or she is overwhelmed by physical pain or illness. In those settings, the compassionate thing to do is to treat those conditions first while also holding the intention that relief leads to more Self-leadership.)

Also, as you become increasingly Self-led—increasingly aware of the ocean and not just the waves—the sense of separation between you and others is reduced. The desire to help people who suffer, as well as those who create suffering, arises spontaneously with the increased appreciation of our interconnectedness. It arises from an intuitive understanding that the suffering of others affects you because, at some level, the other is you. (For most people, this is not a conscious thought—they just feel drawn to do something "more meaningful" with their lives.) These lines from a poem by Buddhist monk Thich Nhat Hanh (1992) capture the compassion that arises from awareness of interconnectedness:

> I am the child in Uganda, all skin and bones, my legs as thin as bamboo sticks, and I am the arms merchant, selling deadly weapons to Uganda. I am the 12-year-old girl, refugee on a small boat, who throws herself into the ocean after being raped by a sea pirate, and I am the pirate, my heart not yet capable of seeing and loving. . . . Please call me by my true names, so I can wake up, and so the door of my heart can be left open, the door of compassion. (pp. 123–124)

Confidence

One reason Self-led people can remain calm and clear in the face of anger is because they trust that no matter what the offended person claims happened, it doesn't mean they are bad or are going to be permanently harmed. We are defensive not because someone is attacking us but rather because the attack is likely to provoke our inner critics, which in turn trigger the worthlessness and terror we accumulated as children. Whatever slight we receive in the present triggers an echo chamber inside us of all the similar hurts we've accumulated from the past. Contemporary events are not what we fear—it's the unending reverberations we'll have to endure that scare us. We dread any incident that confirms our worst fears about ourselves.

As people heal their vulnerable parts, their critics relax and their defenses drop. They feel Self-confident in the sense that their Self has healed those parts and has shown its ability to protect them or to comfort them if they are hurt again. When that's the case, you become less susceptible to former provocations because those things no longer set off your inner echo chambers of past hurts. Instead, you react to the present situation, which may indeed involve danger or pain, with the confidence that you can handle or repair whatever happens. Without overreaction, you take steps to protect yourself and, if the interactions are hurtful, afterward you nurture any of your parts that were hurt.

This is the opposite of our socialized tendency to lock up those hurt parts in our effort to "let it go, don't look back, and just move on." As a result of that philosophy, not only do we accumulate increasing burdens of pain, but we also abandon and isolate the hurting childlike parts of us instead of nurturing them. This strategy leads to less and less confidence in the Self, more vulnerability to the slings and arrows all around us, and, consequently, more protectiveness and sense of being a separate, isolated, lonely individual.

Confidence has another meaning as well in reference to the Self. The knowledge that we're part of the ocean and not just an isolated wave brings with it what might be called a sense of grace. Grace is hard to define and, in Christianity, has traditionally been seen as a gift or blessing from God. In this book, it is associated with the trust that, as one client put it, "I am loved and am love. No matter how bad things seem, it's all okay and will work out the way it should." With this kind of confidence in the essential goodness of life comes an openness to the beauty of the world and a desire to experience that beauty in each moment. It is hard to stay in the present long enough to experience beauty if you lack this kind of confidence because you will be consumed with future plans for your survival or gratification.

People with this kind of confidence are charismatic (yet another word that begins with the letter C), not in the sense of being flashy, clever, or powerful, but in the way the Greeks originally used the word to mean "having the gift of grace." Self-led people possess the charisma of authenticity.

Courage

Clarence Darrow once said, "The most human thing we can do is comfort the afflicted and afflict the comfortable." The Self has the courage to do both.

One might think that the Self's "it's all okay" sense of grace would lead to a detached passivity and acceptance of the injustices of life, but that's not the nature of the Self. The clarity of the Self makes it hard for people to deny injustice and ignore suffering. The compassion of the Self leads people to resist tyranny and fight for the oppressed. The words of the Self bring hope to the hopeless. The energy of the Self seeps into the cracks in the tyrant's walls and gradually erodes them.

Consequently, oppressors attack people whenever they show any signs of Self-leadership. Abusers know that this is the way to control people, which is why virtually all my clients who have been severely sexually abused report that any time they acted in a spirited, spontaneous, or independent way, they were either verbally or physically punished. As a result, they came to fear the Self and keep it out of their body.

Thus, rather than making people passive, confidence and grace have the opposite effect. If we don't fear attack because we aren't as vulnerable, and if we trust that we can handle the consequences, courage is much more accessible to us. If we know that everyone is a wave in the same ocean, we will challenge injustice without judgment. While so far we have emphasized the compassionate, nurturing side of the Self, it is important to remember that the energy of the Self can also be forceful and protective. The martial arts cultivate this protective side of the Self.

We can be forceful without judgment because we know that no matter how an oppressor behaves, he or she has a Self, and our goal is to elicit it, not to further burden him or her with our judgment. As Martin Luther King, Jr., expressed it, "We must realize that the evil deed of the enemy neighbor, the thing that hurts, never quite expresses all that he is. An element of goodness may be found even in our worst enemy." Elsewhere he wrote:

> [Nonviolence] does not seek to defeat or humiliate the opponent, but to win his friendship and understanding. . . . it avoids not only external physical violence but also internal violence of spirit. The nonviolent resister not only refuses to shoot his opponent but he also refuses to hate him. At the center of nonviolence stands the principle of love. . . . if I respond to hate with a reciprocal hate, I do nothing but intensify the cleavage in a broken community. I can only close the gap in a broken community by meeting hate with love. (King, 1994, pp. 211–214)

Courage is not only about being a voice for the disenfranchised. It often takes more courage to recognize the damage we do to others and try to make amends. Clarity helps us to see what we have done and, if we have confidence, to understand that mistakes don't mean we are bad people. We will have the courage to listen to the other's story with curiosity, apologize sincerely, and ask what can be done to repair the damage. The Self-led person not only has the courage to act but also the courage to be accountable for acting.

As a client's Self emerges, he or she increasingly demonstrates another aspect of courage—the willingness to go toward his or her pain and shame. Clients' internal journeys often involve entering the most frightening places in their psyches. There they often wind up witnessing events in their pasts that they had tried to minimize the impact of or forget entirely. In turn, this witnessing often leads to a clearer view of key relationships in the outside world and the determination to change those relationships. These changes sometimes involve financial and emotional risk. It takes courage to look and courage to act on what we see.

Creativity

Many scientists, inventors, and artists report that their inspirations emerged suddenly and fully formed from their unconscious intuition rather than as a result of the labors of their rational minds. Researchers trying to increase creativity in people use techniques like biofeedback to quiet the mind's inner noise and access deeper states (Tony Schwartz, 1995). As writer Anne Lamott (1994) says, "You get your intuition back when you make space for it, when you stop the chattering of the rational mind.

The rational mind doesn't nourish you. You assume that it gives you the truth, because the rational mind is the golden calf that this culture worships, but this is not true. Rationality squeezes out much that is rich and juicy and fascinating" (p. 112). My experience with clients confirms this. They begin to tap into a kind of creative wisdom as their inner noise diminishes and their Self arises. Solutions to longstanding problems emerge, often involving lateral, "out of the box" thinking that was not possible when they were dominated by parts of them that had so many rules about their lives and relationships. It seems that the Self has an innate wisdom about how to create harmony in relationships, whether those relationships are with people around them or with parts inside them. The Self automatically knows how to nurture others and has the clarity, compassion, and courage to do so.

In addition, as people are released from the grip of their inner critics and their concerns about the approval of others, they feel an increased desire and ability to enter what has been called the "flow" state in which creative expression spontaneously flows out of them and they are immersed in the pleasure of the activity (Csikszentmihalyi, 1990). They often begin to feel a sense that they are here to make some type of contribution, and they experience great relief as they move in the direction of making that happen.

To reiterate one theme of this book, however, just quieting the mind is rarely enough. To allow for real Self-expression requires the courage to release all the creative parts we have locked in inner containers. Anne Lamott (1994) knows this:

> But you can't get to any of these truths by sitting in a
> field smiling beatifically, avoiding your anger and damage

and grief. Your anger and damage and grief are the way to the truth. We don't have much truth to express unless we have gone into those rooms and closets and woods and abysses that we were told not to go in to. When we have gone in and looked around for a long while, just breathing and finally taking it in—then we will be able to speak in our own voice and to stay in the present moment. And that moment is home. (p. 201)

Connectedness

As we increasingly embody Self, we will feel a growing sense of connectedness to all the Selves around us. Since it seems to be the nature of the Self to want to strengthen all those connections, people often find themselves spending more time with others in whom they can sense the Self. Correspondingly, they often drop relationships and activities that take them further from sensing those connections.

Lamott's last line above, "And that moment is home," also applies to what you feel when you make a Self-to-Self connection with someone. There is the thirst-quenching sense of finally meeting someone who knows who you really are. There is also the relief of being able to drop the heavy masks with which we try to impress or hide from one another and instead to allow the light of our Self to shine. Author Joan Borysenko (1999) describes a Self-to-Self experience she had with a man she had gotten to know who was dying of AIDS. After a rambling conversation,

Sam looks into my eyes, "I have never felt more peaceful, more safe." I am weeping, safe also in this larger sense of Self, the spiritual self. Sam holds my hands, says something to the effect of how my children must love me, how lucky they are. I stumble over words, know that he has caught a glimpse of something inside of me that is not usually available, even to the people I love the most. It is the relationship between us that has lifted the bushel off the Light. I am my Self only because he is his own Self in this moment. The chatter and doubts and ruminations of ego are gone. We have seen the God in one another. Neither of us cares how we look, how clever our words are. We don't even care if the world ends here and how. We are whole and the story is told. Our lives have had purpose and meaning in this one precious moment. (pp. 164–165)

These sacred, memorable moments are far too rare for most of us. For the Self-led person, however, such connections are not only desired, they are also more possible. This is because Self in one person is a magnet for Self in another. Perhaps a tuning fork is a better metaphor. When you are in Self, the vibrations will set off the other's Self. When in the presence of Self in someone else, your defenses relax as you sense that you won't be judged or controlled, and your own Self naturally arises. Since you are not as afraid of getting hurt, Self-to-Self connections are more possible because you have confidence that you can quickly repair any damage from rejections.

In addition to increasing your connectedness to other people and to your parts (horizontal connectedness), you are likely to feel increased connection to the oneness of the universe or of nature.

I find that people begin to feel more vertically connected to Spirit and to the Earth as their parts relax and their Self is released, and they are drawn to activities and people that further open those doors. The words of eminent neuroscientist Francisco Varela (quoted in Jaworski, 1996, pp. 189–190) capture this state of connectedness:

> When we are in touch with our "open nature," our emptiness, we exert an enormous attraction to other human beings. . . . And if others are in the same space or entering it, they resonate with us and immediately doors are open to us. . . . This state—where we connect deeply with others and doors open—is there waiting for us. It is like an optical illusion. All we have to do is squint and see that it has been there all along, waiting for us. All we have to do is see the oneness that we are.

These are the eight Cs of Self-leadership. There are other C-words, such as consciousness, contentedness, and constancy, that I considered including but believed they were adequately covered in the list above. Other important qualities of the Self, including joy, humor, forgiveness, and gratitude, aren't thoroughly covered above.

A different long list of C-words describes people when their Self is buried beneath the noise and emotion. Some of these include: closed, confused, clouded, clogged, congested, chaotic, cowardly, cautious, compliant, complacent, conceited, computer-like, critical, confronting, craving, cruel, cynical, contemptuous, controlling, coercive, commanding, cocky, compulsive, colluding, conquesting, crafty, clever, and crazy.

EXERCISES

Seeing from the Self

Think of a person in your life to whom you have closed your heart. Perhaps he or she is someone who has hurt you in the past and whom you have decided not to trust again. Maybe it's a person who has qualities that get on your nerves. Once you have a person in mind, imagine that person is in a room and you are outside the room looking in at the person through a window. Notice how you feel as you look at that person. You might feel angry, detached, afraid, or judgmental.

Now shift your focus to that feeling and ask if it would be willing to separate from you a little bit, just for a few moments, while you remain outside the room. It may seem strange to talk to a feeling that way, but for the sake of the exercise, just play along and see how it feels. If, after you ask the feeling to separate from you, you sense a withdrawal of the energy of that feeling, notice what emotion or thought comes up next relative to the person in the room. If the next thing to emerge is not curiosity, acceptance, or compassion—that is, if a feeling or thought arises that wouldn't be coming from your Self—then ask that next feeling or thought to separate as well. If, while doing this exercise, you don't sense an ebbing of protective emotions or thoughts, ask what they are afraid would happen if they did separate. Sometimes those parts of us have good reasons not to want to move aside and leave us vulnerable to that person again. You can reassure them that you won't be going into the room in this imagery exercise or taking any new risks with the person in real life. You just want to get a brief sense of what happens when they let you be present outside the room.

If your protective parts did separate, you may have begun to spontaneously experience qualities of your Self emerging. Perhaps you suddenly felt curious about why the person acted the way he or she did, or you were able to see the situation from the person's perspective and better understand the behavior. Maybe you still didn't want to get near that person but felt less of a need to change him or her. Notice whether the person's image changed, perhaps becoming less repulsive or menacing.

If you are skeptical about doing this exercise yourself because you might have been cued to react this way by reading the chapter, try it on someone you know well who has no awareness of what it's about.

The obvious purpose of this exercise is to get an inkling that you actually have a compassionate, confident essence that can spontaneously arise, even when you face someone you have shut out of your heart. It is also a valuable introduction to the possibility that you can have conversations with emotions and thoughts, and that if you are respectful of them and address their fears, they often become more able to respect your requests. In other words, the exercise can be an opening to a new way of relating to yourself.

. . . .

The path exercise
(You may want to have someone read this exercise to you.)

Get in a relaxed position and take several deep breaths. Imagine you are at the base of a path. It can be any path—one you are familiar with or one you have never been on before. Before you go anywhere on the path, meet with your emotions and thoughts (your parts) at the base and ask that they remain there and allow you to head out on the path without them. If they are afraid to let you go, reassure them that you won't be gone long and that both they and you will benefit from the experience. See if you can arrange for any scared parts to be cared for by those that aren't scared. If parts remain afraid to let you go, don't go, and instead spend some time discussing their fears with them. Exactly what are they afraid will happen if they allow you to go off on your own? If, however, you sense permission to go, head out on the path. Notice as you go whether you are watching yourself on the path or whether you are on it such that you don't see yourself—you just see or sense your surroundings. If you are watching yourself, that's a signal that a part is present. Find the part that's afraid to let you proceed on the path and ask it to relax and return to the base. If it won't, spend time exploring its fears.

As you continue on the path, notice whether you are thinking about anything. If you are, ask those thoughts to return to the base as well so that you increasingly become pure awareness. As you continue on the path, check periodically to see if you are thinking and, if so, gently send the thoughts back. As each part leaves you, notice what happens to your body and mind. Notice the amount of space you sense around you and the kind of energy that flows in your body.

When it feels as if you have spent enough time on the path away from your parts, begin to return to the base. See if it is possible to hold the spaciousness and energy you feel even as you get close to your parts again. When you arrive at the base, meet with your parts and see how they fared without you and what they might need from you. When that process is complete, thank your parts for letting you go if they did. If they didn't, thank them for letting you know they were afraid to let you go. Then take some deep breaths again and follow your breath back to the outside world.

The path exercise, like the previous one, has several purposes. One is to give you a small taste of who you really are—that is, what you are like when you are separated from your ordinary thoughts and emotions. Once away from their parts, most people have a similar experience. They feel lighter, more peaceful and radiant, sometimes joyful, and in the present. People meditate to reach this state; the path is just an imagery device for helping you drop below the surface of your ordinary consciousness into the oceanic Self state. Unlike many other meditative techniques, however, this path exercise makes explicit the negotiations with various parts. Using a mantra or focusing on your breath has a similar effect on parts, lulling them into a relaxed state, but this exercise achieves that end more directly so you have an opportunity to listen to the needs of specific parts.

When people first try this exercise, they often find that many of their parts don't allow them to go. If that happened to you, don't feel bad; it simply means that your parts didn't feel safe enough in this particular context and on this particular day. If your parts didn't let you go, you may have achieved another primary goal of this exercise: to discover the parts that fear being separated from you and learn what they are afraid of. From that discovery, you learn of key parts that need your help and can begin to work with them in ways that are described later in this book.

Some people who set out on the path notice that they are still thinking and discover they've been so identified with certain parts that they considered the parts to be who they were—that is, they mistook one or more parts for their Self. It can be quite disconcerting at first to discover what might be called *Self-imitating parts* (also known as *Self-like parts*) because their existence presents a challenge to your identity. Ultimately, however, it is always valuable and liberating to find these Self-imitating parts and relieve them of their burdens of responsibility.

Along these lines, let me comment on asking you to be on the path rather than watching yourself on it. If you see yourself during an imagery exercise, you're experiencing a part, not your Self. This is because your Self is the one who sees—your ultimate seat of consciousness—so, consequently, you cannot see your Self. If you could, who would be witnessing your Self? In different exercises throughout this book, you will be invited to go inside and interact with parts. When you do, make sure you are not watching yourself do it and instead are actually there.

As you become more familiar with the process of helping parts trust that it is safe to let you separate, you may no longer need an image like the path, may create an image you like better, or may find that just by noticing your parts, they relax and separate. One form of Buddhist meditation guides participants to do just that—simply notice whatever thoughts or feelings arise as you sit and focus on your breath.

As your parts come to trust you more, you will find that your ability to quickly separate and enter the Self state dramatically improves such that you can live increasing amounts of your life from that place. How long that takes depends more on how many burdens (extreme thoughts and emotions from the outside world that were pumped into your system) your parts carry than on how regularly you meditate, which can also help. As we will learn, it is the process of unburdening that releases your Self.

Chapter Three

PARTS

We suffer from a case of mistaken identity. Our culture has sold us a bill of goods about who we really are. Beneath all the inner chatter and emotional turmoil, we are much more than we've been led to believe. But let's return for a moment to that chatter and turmoil. You cannot simply will your Self to be in a leadership role with your parts. Instead, the protective parts that run your life must come to trust that it's safe to permit more Self-leadership. In this chapter, we will get to know parts and learn how they operate.

Let's return to Diane and some other clients in the early 1980s who were describing their extreme emotions and thoughts with this parts language, as if these clients contained entire tribes of warring, autonomous subpersonalities. At that time, I had no personal awareness of any independently functioning characters within me. Like most people, I had been socialized to believe that the mind is unitary, and mine was dominated by an intellectual part that successfully obscured all others. I thought anyone who had autonomous personalities inside them must be crazy. I began worrying that these clients had multiple personality disorder or some other severe pathology.

That perspective lasted until I focused inside and began listening to my own chronic patterns of thinking and feeling. I found that they would talk back to me in ways that I wasn't creating or imagining. My angry part hated the one who criticized me and vice versa. Some of what I called "thinking" revealed itself to be inner battles between those two parts. For example, if I forgot to do something for my wife, the critic would attack me for being inconsiderate or selfish. Then the angry voice would defend me, claiming that she should have reminded me. As I got to know these two, I noticed the same basic argument around any mistake I made—the voices were remarkably consistent. My clients were showing none of the classic symptoms of multiple personality disorder, yet they and I had these characters buzzing around in our minds. And they weren't just making this up or imagining it. From session to session, week to week, and month to month, a striking consistency emerged in the images, stories, and relationships of the parts that couldn't be attributed to clients' imaginations.

Fighting Inner Enemies

After getting past the fear of people's parts, I got excited. What if we all had this collection of internal players that were struggling for control of our souls? What if it were possible to help them get along in the same way I had been helping families? Before I could answer this question, I first had to get to know them better.

That was difficult for me because unlike several of my clients who, when they focused inside, had immediate and clear images of their different parts, I would only have a fuzzy sense of my parts. I find this to be generally true: for some people it's as if they're watching a movie with fascinating characters, and for others like me, it's all quite vague and impressionistic. Nonetheless, as people get to know their parts, they come to realize the complexity of their inner lives. They also realize that they hate some parts and depend on others.

To make this parts discussion more concrete, imagine that you enter a room full of people of different ages. You immediately start sizing up the group and making assumptions about them based on your first impressions. Some of the people seem loud and obnoxious, others look weak and needy, and still others appear to be trying to control the group. Initially you decide to relate only to the ones you find most attractive or most similar to you.

Imagine further that at some point you decide that this crew needs more leadership and you want to provide it for them. It turns out, however, that this group has chronic conflicts between various members. Each time you start to talk to one person, another thinks you're going to side with the first one, so the second person tries to influence you to dislike and stay away from the first one. That constant interference makes it difficult to get to know any of the people as they really are, but over time you are able to have conversations with each member and find that your first impressions were wrong about all of them. The attractive ones have flaws, and the ones you discounted have hidden resources and appeal. As you get to know them beyond their masks or roles, your appreciation of, and relationship with, each of them changes.

That is the experience of many people as they explore their inner worlds. They come to relate to their parts as if they were as real as people in a room, and they find that even the ones they thought were bad respond well to that kind of acceptance. People also find that as they create more harmony inside, many aspects of their external lives improve. But I didn't know about all that in those early days.

To get a clearer picture of my clients' parts, I used an "empty chair" technique in which they would imagine they were talking to one of their parts in an empty chair across from them and then switch seats and give voice to the part in response. For example, I had Diane imagine a bitingly critical part in the empty chair and speak to it. She asked why it was so nasty to her. I then had Diane change chairs and reply as the critic. With a look of arrogance and a deeper voice dripping with disdain, she (as the critic) said, "Because you are totally worthless and incompetent." When she became the critic, I was disconcerted by her dramatic transformation and quickly had her move back to being Diane in her original chair. From there, she feebly argued with the critic but was clearly outmatched. I decided to take over for her. I had Diane become the critic again, and I began pointing out to it various ways in which Diane was competent. Unmoved by my sales pitch, the critic laughed at me scornfully and said, "If you think you can help her, then you're incompetent, too. She's hopeless and in my power."

I, of course, took the bait and entered into a power struggle with this part, which lasted for many sessions. I tried various ways of encouraging Diane to shut the critic out of her mind between sessions—putting it in an imaginary box, thinking only of her positive qualities or accomplishments, repeating affirmations, and telling it to shut up—all of which only made it become more aggressive and powerful. Diane was getting increasingly depressed, and I was worried. Finally I cried uncle. I told the part that I realized neither I nor Diane could control it and that we would stop trying. I wondered, however, why it was so committed to making her feel worthless. What was it afraid would happen if she felt good about herself? The critic softened visibly and said that Diane would become the fat, lazy person that she wanted to be.

Once I let go of the need to change this part and just became curious, it could let down its guard and reveal its predicament. The critic described how hard it worked to motivate Diane. It felt responsible for getting her to look and perform perfectly so she wouldn't be rejected. It told of other parts of her that were extremely indulgent that would make her binge eat or lie in bed if they took over. It also told of the wounded, childlike parts that felt so rejected by other children when Diane was young because she was pudgy. The critic was trying desperately to protect those wounded parts and to stave off the indulgent ones. It was exhausted from the struggle and longed to rest.

This encounter with Diane's critic was a tremendous lesson for me. With this part and others like it in other clients, I had been "judging the book by its cover." I had identified these parts with the roles they had been forced into. I had assumed that rageful parts were just bundles of angry emotion; parts that binged on food or alcohol contained the clients' impulsiveness; parent-like critics were internal representations of parents; and so on. Because I thought they were the way they first seemed and had little capacity for change, I encouraged clients to fight with them. Diane wasn't the only client losing the internal battle I had instigated. But when I could help other clients drop the war and become curious about these apparent demons, the parts all told stories similar to the story told by Diane's critic.

The following excerpt transcribed from a session with another client, Patricia, provides a clearer picture of how work with people's parts can proceed. Patricia was a sophisticated, accomplished woman in her early fifties, so I was surprised by the problem she wanted to work on.

PATRICIA: Well, something that always bugs me is a fear of appearing stupid. Sometimes it doesn't bother me so much—it's like background noise and I ignore it. But in other situations, it takes over so much that I'm paralyzed and can't speak.

SCHWARTZ: What kinds of situations?

PATRICIA: Usually when I'm with a woman who is very, very intelligent. Usually I feel as if I don't have anything at all to contribute in that situation, and I just go catatonic.

SCHWARTZ: Okay, so you want to be free of that kind of paralysis or fear?

PATRICIA: If I could be free of that reaction, my whole life would be so much better! Because even though I can kind of deal with it—I can get it to go away sometimes—it's still just eroding me, you know, pulling me down, keeping me from saying things I know. I would love to change it! It's been with me for a long time!

Like the clients I described in the first chapter, Patricia has formed a chronically dysfunctional relationship with this paralyzing fear. She has done everything she can think of to try to get rid of it, but nothing has worked. What she has never thought to do—just listen to it rather than try to eradicate it—is what it needs.

SCHWARTZ: Do you have any fear of trying to get to know it?

PATRICIA: No, I'm curious about it, and I'm mad at it, you know—angry at the power it has had in my life.

SCHWARTZ: Okay, let's go ahead and focus on it, on the part that paralyzes you in those situations, and just see where you find it in or around your body.

PATRICIA (closing her eyes and directing her attention inside): The first sense I get is of something behind me, like with a harness on me, holding me back, kind of saying, "How dare you!"

SCHWARTZ: Okay. So let's focus right back there . . . and tell me how you feel toward the part now.

When I ask, "How do you feel toward that part?" I'm trying to get a sense of how much of her Self is present by listening to the content and tone of her response.

PATRICIA: My first reaction is to say, "Get away from me," you know, "Get off of me," but I'm also a bit curious as to why it wants to hold me back.

In this response, I hear a different part of her ("Get away from me"), but I also sense the curiosity of the Self beginning to emerge as she separates from and focuses on the part that's holding her back. I'll see if the part that wants this part to get away will step back and let her Self emerge more.

SCHWARTZ: So the part that wants the paralyzing part to get away from you—ask that part to just be patient and let us follow your curiosity, and we'll just get to know the paralyzing one a little bit and see why it's doing this to you. Is that okay?

PATRICIA: The one that wants to get away from it feels angry. It's impatient.

SCHWARTZ: Okay, but is it willing to let us do this and not interfere?

PATRICIA: It says, "It better work."

SCHWARTZ: Or what?

PATRICIA: Or he's going to take over again. But I say to him, "Your technique has never worked."

SCHWARTZ: And what does he say to that?

PATRICIA: He's a little humbled by having that pointed out.

SCHWARTZ: So he acknowledges that that's true.

PATRICIA: Right. So he backs off.

By now, I can tell by the way she's talking that Patricia has fully entered the inner world of her parts. To an observer, it looks as if she's in a hypnotic trance, but people describe it more as though they are in the middle of a dream talking to different characters in the dream who are talking back to them.

SCHWARTZ: So, how are you feeling now toward this part that's scolding you and holding you back?

PATRICIA: I'm wondering why it would do that.

SCHWARTZ: Now how do you feel toward the paralyzing part?

PATRICIA: Like somehow I know it very well, but I can't put any content around it.

SCHWARTZ: It's familiar.

PATRICIA: (beginning to cry) Yeah, it's familiar. But I'm afraid if you ask me another question, I won't be able to answer it.

SCHWARTZ: That's okay. There's a feeling that comes with that? What's the feeling?

PATRICIA: Uh huh. Of . . . a bit of compassion toward it. Like when you see an old friend.

As Patricia gets closer to the part and isn't so angry at it, she can see it more as it really is, which evokes her natural compassion for it.

SCHWARTZ: Okay, so could you show the part that you feel that way toward it?

PATRICIA: Let's see . . . Yeah, I can.

SCHWARTZ: How is it reacting?

PATRICIA: It seems a little bit like a dog—a dog that hasn't been fed for a long time that wants to move toward a person who's offering it food, but it's afraid because it has been beaten too many times.

SCHWARTZ: Yeah. So, is it possible to just reassure it until it's willing to trust you a little more?

PATRICIA: It's so strange because I've hated it for so long. I've been angry at it for so long.

SCHWARTZ: I know. But, as you said to that other part, that
   didn't work.

PATRICIA: Right . . . So, it feels as if I'm moving a little closer
   to it, and it's moving a little closer to me. I seem to feel
   so much pity for it. And it's so curious about my reaction
   because it's so used to my reaction being, "Get out of here!"
   So it's hesitant about my . . . it's suspicious, as if any minute,
   I'm going to turn around and hit it with a stick or something.

*As she describes this scene, it sounds as though Patricia sees herself
getting closer to the dog. When people are seeing themselves doing the
work, it means that their Self is watching some other part do it for
them. I check on that and ask her to really be with the dog rather than
watch herself with it.*

SCHWARTZ: Patricia, do you see yourself getting closer to it,
   or are you there getting closer to it?

PATRICIA: I can't quite tell anymore. At first I thought it was one,
   and then I thought it was the other. It goes back and forth.

SCHWARTZ: Okay. Just ask your parts to see if they'll let you
   be there.

PATRICIA: Just be with it?

SCHWARTZ: Yes.

PATRICIA: I see parts of myself back up, and I begin to feel myself
   moving closer to it, and then I jump out and I think, *I've got
   to watch this, I've got to see it.*

SCHWARTZ: That's the one. The one that makes you jump out and want to watch—ask that part to really separate and, if necessary, to go into another room or something.

PATRICIA: Okay. I've got this assessment that I've got to watch the part like a technique I've got, like I should observe it.

SCHWARTZ: Yeah, that part that's telling you that, that holds that rule, that technique—let's see if it will step out.

PATRICIA: Okay. Okay. I feel a little frightened to just be here with the part that's holding me back rather than to be observing myself doing it. I don't know what it would be like to just experience it.

SCHWARTZ: Yeah. The one who's frightened about that . . . see if it's willing to trust you and me on this one, and I can let that part know that it's better to be there. It's better for the part, and it's better for the whole system.

PATRICIA: Okay, I'm just going to trust your experience. Okay.

SCHWARTZ: So, you're there with the part? How are you feeling?

PATRICIA: Calm and just glad to be here.

SCHWARTZ: Now can you just reassure this part that you care about it, that you're not going to hit it, you're not going to yell at it?

PATRICIA: (with a lot of emotion) I allow it to notice that the other parts have stepped back. I allow it to notice that I've not been the one to hit it. Or hate it. Or even be afraid of it.

SCHWARTZ: And how is it reacting?

PATRICIA: Like it rests . . . like it rests. I feel as if I have to practice this because I'm not used to being with it or even just seeing it. I'm used to just trying to get rid of it.

As Patricia found, if we don't attack our parts, they can drop their guard. Then we can get to know who they really are and why they do what they do, and then we can help them change.

Not all IFS sessions go as smoothly as Patricia's. She had worked enough on herself previously that her parts already had a great deal of trust in the leadership of her Self. This was reflected in how quickly they were willing to step back when she asked them to. As was evident in the session, this stepping-back process releases more and more of her Self and, as that happens, she increasingly leads the process. The parts that are asked to step back aren't relegated to any kind of exile. They are just being asked not to interfere while her Self gets to know the paralyzing part until it is healed. Later they can share their reactions, voice their concerns, and, if they are ready, have their turn to heal. As each part drops its extreme role, all the parts begin to change their relationships with one another, eventually becoming an integrated, harmonious group. As I hope is clear from the transcript, I encourage people to work with their parts as if they were inner people. But what are they really?

The Normal Multiplicity of the Mind

My clients were experiencing their parts as if they were internal people—that is, as full-range personalities that had been forced into protective roles they didn't like but were afraid to leave. Was it possible that was who they really were? I was being led by my clients into foreign territory—toward a radical reconception of the nature of their minds, my mind, the mind.

Later I learned that I was not the first to be led into this territory. A number of intrapsychic explorers encountered what I call the *normal multiplicity of the mind* long before I did. Roberto Assagioli, an Italian psychiatrist, deserves credit as the first in the West to recognize this phenomenon and develop an approach based on working with subpersonalities, which he called *psychosynthesis.* I was excited to see how similar his understanding of subpersonalities was to what my clients' parts were teaching me about themselves. Carl Jung (1962) also recognized the multiplicity inside himself and his clients, and used a process called *active imagination* to gain access to that inner world. Of the inhabitants he found there, he said, "There are things in the psyche which I do not produce, but which produce themselves and have their own life. . . . they always have a certain degree of autonomy, a separate identity of their own. Their autonomy is a most uncomfortable thing to reconcile oneself to. . . ." (pp. 181, 183). Other theorists from fields like hypnotherapy and traumatology have realized that subpersonalities are not exclusive to people with multiple personality disorder.

Neurobiologists and computer scientists have recognized the multiplicity of the normal mind and have come up with their own explanations and models. Computer scientists find that parallel processing computers, which consist of many small processors all working independently on a problem, operate more similarly to the human mind than the older serial processing computers. Neuroscientists speak of "states of mind" or "modules" as discrete clusters of related mental processes that are linked into cohesive submind-like states. The idea is that, for efficiency's sake, the brain is designed to form these clusters—connections among certain memories, emotions, ways of perceiving the world, and behaviors—which stay together as internal units that can be activated when needed. For example, neuropsychiatrist Daniel Siegel (1999) writes that a fearful state of mind clusters together ". . . a state of heightened caution, focal attention, behavioral hypervigilance, memories of past experiences of threat, models of the self as victim in need of protection, and emotional arousal alerting the body and mind to prepare for harm . . ." (pp. 208–209). Once such traits are linked, they come forth together in the face of future threats. Other clusters are evoked by different stimuli. From this perspective, multiplicity is inherent in the way the brain evolved to efficiently handle changes in our environments. These clusters then take on inner lives of their own.

Despite these reports from a wide variety of sources, the idea of the mind as containing a host of discrete, autonomous characters with an entire network of relationships remains, as Jung wrote, ". . . a most uncomfortable thing to reconcile oneself to." The idea of normal multiplicity has remained on the fringes of the mental health establishment and the culture at large. We may talk about our inner child, our superego, or our temper, but very few of us consider those to be literal inner beings. Instead, we think of them as metaphors for emotional states or as aspects of our unitary personalities. Assagioli's work remains marginalized, and while Jung's has had a sizable and growing impact on our culture, the subpersonality facet of his thinking is far less acknowledged or understood. We remain single-mindedly attached to the idea of having a single mind, clinging to the belief that the only people with more than one are those poor souls who have multiple personality disorder. It is not uncommon for clients to ask fearfully, "Do you think I'm Sybil?" after their first internal journey.

As we get to know the shamanic traditions of different indigenous groups, it is becoming increasingly clear that the idea of the mind as unitary is a relatively recent invention of "civilized" society. Indigenous cultures throughout the world were familiar and comfortable not only with a spirit world but also with an inner realm inhabited by many different voices and characters. It may be that the idea of the normal mind as multiple is less a radical departure from established knowledge than it is a return to age-old wisdom from which "established knowledge" radically departed.

This is not to minimize the difficulty of shifting our beliefs toward normal multiplicity. Despite accumulating evidence from client after client, it took me at least five years after those early explorations with Diane until I could fully accept that possibility. In contrast to people like Diane and Patricia, I still don't experience myself that way intuitively unless I deliberately focus my awareness inside. In my ordinary state of consciousness, I don't notice the subtle shifts in perspective and demeanor or the habitual voices as parts come and go. All of that blends together into a mosaic of my experience, and I identify with the gestalt of the mosaic, unaware of the pieces—until, that is, one of the pieces gets upset and takes over. Then I can sense how much of a different person I become.

For example, can you remember a time when a family member or intimate partner did something to hurt you, and you got angry with him or her? How did your thinking change, not just about that person, but in general? How did your vision, your posture and movements, and your voice change? If you are like me, it was as if your body was temporarily hijacked by a different person. I begin thinking in terms of black and white, good and bad. I feel younger, more impulsive, and more energetic. My love or empathy for the other person vanishes; I can only see my side of things, and I have an overwhelming desire to get my way. I can be reckless, with little concern for the consequences of my actions or words. My opponent changes physically, looking uglier and more repulsive. I suddenly become demonstrative, gesturing broadly with my arms to emphasize my points. I tend to whine loudly and speak with contempt or condescension. In other words, I transform from a reasonable facsimile of a human being into a hormonal, self-centered adolescent boy.

Once I focused on that anger and asked questions of it, I learned that it was indeed an adolescent personality in me that not only was angry but also felt hurt and afraid. He believed he had to protect me from being hurt by people I got close to, so he led with his anger in times of danger. However, that anger is not his essence—it just comes with the territory of his protective role. He stands heroically in front of the younger parts of me that carry the pain from past rejections, and he counters my scared parts that are afraid to stand up to anyone. If you are able to focus on your anger with an attitude of curiosity, you may be surprised to learn that it, too, is far more than just a bundle of emotion. You may even find yourself feeling compassion and gratitude for it.

A system of full-range inner personalities

Thus, the term *parts* sells the phenomenon short. I use that word because it's more user-friendly than *subpersonality*. Everyone says things like, "A part of me wants to go to work today, but another part would rather stay in bed." But I am talking about full-range inner personalities, not unlike "alters" found in multiple personality disorder. Because of the severity of abuse they endured as children, people given that diagnosis have parts that are so isolated from and polarized with one another that when one takes over, a dramatic shift in demeanor occurs, sometimes as well as a loss of memory of what happened when other parts were there. Such clients needed extreme inner compartmentalization to survive. Those of us whose childhoods weren't filled with horrible experiences have parts that relate more harmoniously, so we feel and look more integrated. In this context, having an integrated personality does not signify an absence of parts. It means that they get along and work together better, but they don't disappear. Parts surface and withdraw, and we sense their presence, but our identity doesn't shift as dramatically because the rest of us is present while that happens.

As my view of parts shifted from unidimensional (such as the angry one) to multidimensional (a hurt adolescent personality forced into the role of the angry one), I was able to use my training in family therapy to further understand their predicaments. For example, I had a client, Billy, a fifteen-year-old with multicolor hair and many body piercings, who was getting into trouble at school and whose parents said he always seemed angry at home. As a family therapist, I was taught to inquire about his family history and his relationships with other family members and peers in order to understand his behavior in context. In doing that, I learned that Billy felt protective of his mother and younger sister because his father had been abusive to them in the past. In light of that history, it makes sense that Billy would have been forced into the role of the angry protector.

In general, we are not socialized to think in terms of interconnected systems. Ours is an individualistic culture in which people are assumed to be responsible for their behavior. Pregnant teenagers are judged to be immoral; unemployed people, lazy; drug addicts, hedonistic. We rarely look for connections and often consider any that are suggested to be excuses for irresponsible behavior. Billy was seen as one of the bad kids at school and diagnosed as having a conduct disorder. Everyone was judging his book by its cover.

This process of trying to understand how a person's behavior is connected to relationships with other people or to past events, rather than judging the person solely on the way he or she looks or acts, is called systems thinking. Family therapy brought systems thinking into a mental health field that had previously been dominated by the Freudian and medical models, which diagnosed and treated people with little consideration for the social contexts of their problems.

With my background in systems thinking, I began trying to understand how the role of a client's part was connected to its relationships with other parts, just as I had connected Billy's anger to his position in his family. As mentioned earlier, asking Diane's critic about what it was afraid would happen if it didn't make her feel so bad revealed that two sets of inner relationships were keeping it in the critic role. The critic feared that if it didn't constantly push Diane, indulgent parts of her would take over and make her fat and lazy. The critic also feared that the vulnerable, childlike parts it protected would be hurt because she'd be rejected. Just as Billy felt forced to remain in his angry role because he was in conflict with his father and protecting his mother and sister, so

Diane's critic was constrained from changing by being conflicted with some parts while protecting others.

What does all this mean for you and your internal relationships? First, it underscores the fact that the way you understand your parts will determine how you relate to them. If you see them merely as internalized beliefs or unidimensional emotional states, you have little reason to listen to or open your heart to them. If, on the other hand, you believe they are multidimensional, autonomous personalities, you'll be much more likely to approach them with curiosity and compassion.

Second, it means that your mind is an intricate system. Your parts have relationships with one another that resemble the relationships between people in families. Many of your parts can't change until the parts they protect or are embattled with have changed first. If you stay curious with a part, you will learn about the reasons it's afraid to change and that sometimes those reasons are realistic. I have worked, for example, with many inner-city kids who couldn't afford to drop their protective wall of diffidence and bravado in their neighborhoods because others would attack them if they were ever vulnerable. We could, however, negotiate with those protectors so the kids could be more selective regarding when their walls were really needed after the kids began demonstrating that they could care for their vulnerable parts.

Polarization

If your mind is a system of parts, how do systems operate? One principle of human systems is that differences tend to escalate into polarizations. Have you ever been in an argument in which you found yourself taking a position that you didn't really believe in just to counter your partner's extreme position? Maybe you defended Bill Clinton's affairs just because your father-in-law hated him so much, even though you really thought Clinton was wrong. You thought that if you backed down at all, your father in-law's wrong-headed politics would prevail. You refused to give in until he did! This is called polarization: each partner takes a position that is the polar opposite to, or competitive with, the other out of fear that something terrible will happen if they don't. It happens in human systems at all levels. Parents become enemies, siblings become rivals, inner parts become antagonists.

Psychiatrist Paul Watzlawick and his colleagues (1974) used a nautical metaphor (which I will embellish) to illustrate polarization in systems. They conjured an image of ". . . two sailors hanging out of either side of a sailboat in order to steady it: the more the one leans overboard, the more the other has to compensate for the instability created by the other's attempts at stabilizing the boat, while the boat itself would be quite steady if not for their acrobatic efforts at steadying it" (p. 36). Both sailors have left their preferred, valuable roles and are in positions that are destructive to the boat, making it susceptible to capsizing. Both are also rigidly limited in their positions. Each has to remain extreme in proportion to the extremity of the other. Each can move only in relation to the moves of the other. The irony is that neither likes the role he or she is in and both wish to return to harmony, yet each has valid reason to fear the consequences of unilaterally leaving his or her position. The ship *would* tip over if he or she moved in.

Each sailor is correct in believing that if he or she moves in, the boat will topple because the other will still be leaning out. The only solution is for both of them to move in at the same time.

Since they don't trust each other, the only way for that to happen is for a third party they both trust to assure each that if one moves in, the other will as well. If they have a trusted captain, he or she can coax both sailors to come down off the railing simultaneously. Once released from the strain and constraint of the polarization, each sailor can then move about the boat freely and can return to a valuable and enjoyable role, trusting the captain to steer a safe and mutually beneficial course.

To pursue our version of this analogy, let us return to Diane. Many of Diane's parts were polarized in this way. As I described earlier, she constantly heard from a critical voice that pushed her to work hard and be perfect. If she sat still for any time, this striving part would criticize her for being lazy and remind her of all the things that needed to be done. I had Diane ask this critical striver what it was afraid would happen if it did not keep her in constant motion, running her to the point of exhaustion. It said she would sit around all day and binge on food until she became fat. Diane reported that she had been a chubby child and adolescent, and had suffered for it. She acknowledged having a part that wanted to binge eat, and she had been fighting it constantly since having lost weight in college.

In its own defense, Diane's binge part told her that because the striver was so dominating, it had to seize any moment when she was exhausted to bring Diane to a grinding halt, and it binged to deal with the tension from the critic's pressure around food. Then, as soon as her binge was over, the critic would start attacking her for being such a pig and would prod her back into a frantic treadmill state. Thus, each of Diane's polarized parts believed that if it became less extreme, the other would totally take over and, in effect, sink her boat. These parts were deadlocked. Neither could become less extreme without the assurance that the other would follow suit, and each would resist such a suggestion until it received that assurance. The two parts were in a battle over her safety, both thinking that the other was bringing her down.

Lacking this understanding of her inner system, many people around Diane, including another therapist, had given her the common-sense prescription, "Why don't you slow down and stop running yourself ragged?" They didn't know that they were inadvertently siding with her binge part and, consequently, making her striving critic all the more extreme. Until you understand the nature of polarization, you will continue to make such mistakes. Just like people in a family or countries in international politics, polarized parts cannot and will not change unilaterally.

As is made clear by the boat example, however, achieving harmony and balance between crew members is not possible without effective leadership. Fortunately, everyone already has a capable internal leader. When Diane was able to interact with each part from her Self, each came to trust her, and her Self was able to help her striver and her binge part meet together and end their battle for her soul. Ultimately, the striving part shifted into the role of advisor, setting reasonable goals and strategizing their achievement. As the binge part realized it no longer had to save Diane from the striving critic, it became a calm voice reminding her to relax.

The end of this polarization and the striving and bingeing that came with it gave Diane access to the vulnerable, childlike parts and their burdens of sadness that all the activity distracted her from. Since the two protectors didn't resume their battling, she was able to stay present with the sadness long enough to learn of its origin and heal the part that carried it.

I found that parts that had plagued other clients for years were trapped in similar predicaments involving polarization and protection. Just as for Billy, something would have to be done about his father for him to soften, polarized parts of other clients couldn't change until other things changed first. I had been getting my clients into power struggles with these parts that they were doomed to lose because the parts couldn't back down. Each of these polarized parts believed the safety of the internal system depended on it staying in its role. Before Diane's critic could totally lighten up, she had to show it that she could protect the vulnerable parts herself and that she would not allow the indulgent ones to take over.

Stuck in the past

The experience with Diane's critic produced a shift in my approach. Rather than trying to forcefully reorganize clients' inner systems, I became increasingly curious about them. To really understand parts, I made an effort to drop all my presumptions about the nature of thought and emotion, and allow myself to be educated by my clients. I interviewed hundreds of clients' parts, trying to remain open and curious even with the ones that wanted to harm my client or others. It became clear that the roles of many of these parts were directed not only by their protective or polarized positions in the system, but also by beliefs and emotions that seemed irrational. One client's angry part sensed danger all around him, even though he lived in as safe an environment as anyone I knew. Another client's suicidal part was convinced that she had to die because she was evil. Still another client had a part that believed he was unlovable despite having many people in his life who clearly loved him.

Instead of challenging such beliefs, I began asking where the parts got those ideas. Immediately following that question, many clients would begin seeing images from their pasts. For some, it was as if they were watching specific scenes from a movie of their own childhood. The scenes were often of traumas— rejections, humiliations, physical or sexual abuse, and frightening or shameful events. Usually these were not forgotten memories but rather events that had been minimized, trivialized, or obscured in these clients' life narratives. Several clients became upset as they watched, weeping and cowering as if they had been pulled into the scenes and were reliving them. I wasn't sure what to do as this was happening. In those early days, I was not totally comfortable in the presence of intense emotion, whether my own or that of clients or family members. As clients approached my threshold of emotional comfort, I was afraid they would be overwhelmed with feelings to the point of no return and that they would enter some kind of no-exit state of despair.

It's no coincidence that I had been afraid of the same thing happening to me if I got too close to my own exiled feelings. Then, in the mid-1990s, a crisis in my life wrenched forth some of those hurt and lonely parts of me, and I was forced to get to know and value them. After that, I was much better able to stay with my clients while they experienced intense emotion. Before that personal work, however, when clients were becoming agitated or tearful, I would ask them to step out of their trauma scenes and would have them watch from a more detached state. Clients were often able to do that, but some shut down entirely and had trouble returning to the scenes to complete the work.

Once a part was able to show when in a client's past it picked up an irrational belief or emotion, the belief or emotion suddenly seemed far less irrational. Given what had happened to the client, it made perfect sense that he or she would have thought or felt that way during that time. Somehow a part of my client continued to carry the ideas, emotions, and sensations from those earlier episodes, even though many years had elapsed and the person was no longer in the situation. It was as if these parts of my clients were stuck in the past, frozen in a dreadful time—as if what had happened back then was, for those parts, still happening or likely to happen. It also seemed as if those parts still carried old messages they received about themselves and the world. Many clients felt relief after witnessing their parts' stories. They had been confused for years by what seemed to their rational minds to be crazy compulsions, fears, yearnings, or world views. Now they understood the reasons for those feelings, beliefs, and behaviors.

Good Parts Liberated from Bad Roles

More significant than this, however, was the reaction of the parts to finally feeling understood. It was as if they had been trying to tell their stories for many years but couldn't get through. All they seemed to need was for the person's Self to understand what happened and to appreciate how bad it was. Once that had taken place, many of these parts immediately transformed. Clients reported that their image and experience of the part changed. It was as if a part had released a burden that, like a computer chip or curse, had been governing its existence. Many parts became joyful, as if liberated from bondage like the flying monkeys in *The Wizard of Oz* after the Wicked Witch melted. After being unburdened, many parts just wanted to play, dance, or rest. Surprisingly, others took on a role opposite to the one they had been in. For example, Diane's critic wanted to become a supportive cheerleader that encouraged her to do her best.

Witnessing these transformations in clients' parts led me to the view of parts that I hold now—as full-range inner personalities that accompany us in life to provide all manner of valuable service. Some are young and full of innocence, awe, and delight. They add a robustness to our existence, helping us play, create, relax, and enjoy intimacy. Others are good at sizing up situations and people. Like valued advisors, they can plan and problem solve. Still others bring perseverance during difficulties and the strength to face challenges. Some are very sexual, while others are more interested in artistic pleasures.

It's as if we each have within us a collection of people of various ages, temperaments, and talents who, when they aren't burdened by the past or fighting with each other, can assist in any activity. When our internal families are relating harmoniously, a part with a specific talent will come forward when that talent is needed, and others will recede. For example, I have worked with sports figures to help them find a part that has extraordinary athletic prowess so that when they perform, it can enter their body reliably and consistently rather than only occasionally. My own athletic part is so effective partly because it doesn't worry about what anyone thinks about my performance, so I'm able to enter the flow of a game with minimal performance anxiety. That kind of imperviousness is not useful, however, when I'm making up with my partner after an argument. In that context, things go well when my parts that are sensitive to how I've affected others show up and the impervious athletic guy steps back.

Ideally, your Self is present for every activity and interaction, and the appropriate parts are close by, offering suggestions, blending their emotions or abilities with your Self, or sometimes even fully taking over your body. In this ideal scenario, when a part does take over, it's with permission of the Self rather than being an automatic reaction to step in and protect. It can be great fun to fully embody playful parts, and it can also be healing at times to give grieving parts full expression. Thus, a Self-led person is not detached from the world, with emotions always in abeyance. Instead, such a person drinks deeply from the bittersweet fountain of life while simultaneously maintaining a center of equanimity.

If you are like me, you are far from that ideal. There are some challenging contexts in which I am almost always able to remain Self-led, other times when Self-leadership is inconsistent, and still other situations, such as when my partner is furious with me, when I usually lose Self-leadership. Her anger triggers parts of me that are stuck at different points in my childhood and carry intense burdens of fear, shame, rage, or self-hate. When any of those parts gets upset, it can flood my consciousness to the point that my Self is temporarily obscured and I think, feel, and act as that part. These are very dark times for me because I can't see beyond the hopelessness and limiting perspective of these parts and feel overwhelmed by their emotions. I become the young boy I once was, afraid of my father's spanking or my mother's scolding and certain that my relationship with each of them has been irretrievably destroyed. I'm awash in a sea of feelings and experience no "I" in the storm. Fortunately, since the time I mentioned in the mid-1990s when I healed some parts, these episodes no longer last as long, and my Self pops back to the surface more quickly than before. While the dark nights of my soul are shorter, they are still unpleasant. Depending on which part takes over, I might shut down and sulk or lash out at my partner in a verbal counterattack. I can lose any sense of my love for her in the swirl of anger and hurt, and begin to wonder why I ever got together with her. Inevitably her parts are further triggered by mine, and we are off to the races.

Given how much parts can interfere in our lives and make us feel horrible, it makes sense that we wish we could get rid of them. It's hard to see any value in an inner voice that constantly berates you or a fear in your gut that makes you withdraw. These parts have such devastating power over us that the natural impulse is to hate and fight them. And it's true: they often are destructive in their present state. I am not asking you to accept your depression or learn to cope with your racism. I'm suggesting that if you relate to any part differently, it will unload its destructive burdens and transform into something valuable. As difficult as this may be to believe, even the most diabolical of them is a good part forced into a bad role. I feel like the Will Rogers of this phenomenon; I never met a part that ultimately I didn't like. And I've met some nasty parts—some that wanted to kill my client and others that had molested children. Even those apparent inner demons, when approached with nonjudgmental curiosity, revealed the reasons that had forced them into those roles and their shame at what they had done. Even those very extreme parts eventually transformed.

Unburdened clients

What happens to people as they begin to reorganize their inner system and lead with their Self? Some clients take a new look at their lives and experience what poet David Whyte calls a form of "internal sticker shock." They realize the price they have been paying for fear-based decisions they made in the past that left them in a career, lifestyle, or marriage with little room for their Self or newfound parts. They follow their passions into uncharted waters.

For many other clients, however, the changes in their external lives are less dramatic. They find ways to enrich or slow down the lives they already lead. They often add creative endeavors, time in nature, new relationships, or service-based volunteer activities, and they subtract things that were done primarily to soothe or distract from their pain and shame. They become less obsessed with achievement, money, computers, time-management, and appearance, and move toward wanting to just be with people or with themselves. They ride more smoothly over bumps in the rocky road of life that used to send them reeling because they now seem to have better shock absorbers.

For some clients, rather than leaving partners or occupations they once blamed for their turmoil, the inner work brings a new appreciation of their situation. When these clients finally listen inside to what they really need, it has nothing to do with a different spouse, job, or body. Simply embracing the parts of them that had been stranded in the dark forests of their psyches lifts the cloud that had shrouded their souls. As they become more accepting of themselves, they can accept the parts of their partners that resemble their own exiles. Lifelong cravings and obsessions evaporate, and they feel more present in their lives because, literally, more of them is present.

What does it mean to be more present in one's life? Consider this entry from a client's journal. Holly Dunn is a single parent with a son, Josh, and two daughters.

Saturday night, Josh had his friend over to spend the night. They asked me to take them bike riding at the park. It sounded good—I wanted to go. The three of us set off on our bikes. We rode up the big hill that took us to the park and then down into the parking lot with its wide-open spaces and small hills and valleys. The boys' smiles and peals of laughter floated through the evening air. A peaceful contentment flowed through my veins.

The next day, Josh and I went to the lake. It was a hot day, the best kind for swimming. I held his feet as he dove off my hands. In the deep waters of the lake under the high quarry walls, we swam after each other in endless games of tag. All of me was there with Josh in the water—I didn't want or need to be anywhere else.

Monday, Josh asked if he could have his special night, for it means so much to him and I always feel there should be more special nights. It was a perfect time for it, with his sisters gone. He asked to go to Red Lobster, his favorite place. The boy loves crab. I was worried about the money but decided I wanted him to have his night the way he wanted it. He relished every bite of his crab. Then we went to see Tarzan. I loved being with him, pleasing him. He is nine and still likes to hold my hand, still cuddles with me.

I love it when he smiles, when he is happy.

All this may seem simple and ordinary to someone else. But for me, it is not. It is what I have longed for—more than anything else—for so long. I have wanted my love for my children to flow freely, spontaneously—I have wanted to take delight in them, to simply have fun being with them. I have wanted to spend time with them—not because I should, not out of obligation, but with genuine enjoyment. I have wanted to be fully there with them, without distraction or preoccupation. And though I am almost afraid to say it for fear of jinxing it, it is starting to happen. It snuck up on me during the bike riding and the next day swimming and during Josh's special night. It was flowing, just like I'd always wanted—my love and pleasure in being with him felt as natural as a soft and gentle rain.

These weren't new activities for Holly. What was new was the absence of the usual inner yammering about what she needed to do the next day, what Josh was doing that was wrong or dangerous, how bad she was for not doing this more often, and so on, and the presence of parts of her that loved to play, loved the feeling of her body in action, and loved just being with Josh. It's that combination—the absence of yammering and the presence of formerly exiled parts of us—that can bring the love of life we yearn for.

The Possibility of Goodness

This journey of discovery with my clients has led to astounding conclusions about who we really are. Not only are we much more at our core than we could imagine, but the very aspects of us that we thought proved our worthlessness are actually diamonds in the rough. We are inherently good, through and through.

Since my skepticism only began to abate after years of seeing these uplifting assumptions confirmed again and again, I don't expect you to accept these ideas just because I say they're true. No one should conclude one way or another until they have done their own inner explorations. As Buddha said, "Do not believe in the strength of traditions even if they have been held in honor for many generations and in many places; do not believe anything because many people speak of it; do not believe in the strength of sages of old times. . . . After investigation, believe that which you yourself tested and found reasonable." However, because we have all been marinating in our culture's negative biases about the human psyche, it is difficult for any of us to explore with an open, curious, beginner's mind. This book attempts to level the playing field so that as you explore your inner world, you consider supplanting the culturally conditioned expectation of pathology with the possibility of goodness.

—————————— EXERCISE ——————————

Getting to know a part

Clear some time and find a comfortable, private space. Then select an emotion, thought pattern, or inner voice you would like to get to know. In the early stages of exploration, it's best to start with one about which you don't have terribly extreme feelings. If you need help thinking of one, you might scan the list from the exercises in Chapter 1. When you have made your selection, begin to focus on that voice, thought, or feeling and notice where it seems to be located in or around your body. If you don't find a specific location, that's fine, but if you do, it can help to focus on that place in your body as you continue.

Notice how you feel toward the part of you from which that voice, thought, or feeling is coming. If you feel anything besides curiosity, acceptance, or compassion toward the part, find the other parts that are giving you those feelings or beliefs about the original one and see if they are willing to trust you and step back. If they do step back and you do feel curious toward the original part, take some time to be with it and see what it might want to share with you.

Chapter Four

Exiles, Managers, and Firefighters

You may have noticed that the clients I have mentioned thus far tend to have two kinds of parts—some that are protecting their system and others that are more vulnerable and are being protected. In this chapter, I will present a map for better understanding the different types of parts. Because we have all been hurt and socialized in similar ways, our internal systems organize into similar patterns. Protective parts of you have been forced into roles that are similar to parts of mine. The difference in how we operate is largely related to differences in the roles of the parts that dominate us. I tend to be shy, so the part of me that discourages social risks is strong. It's forever telling me I'll be rejected, so I shouldn't try. I also have a part that likes people and can be quite outgoing. In that polarization, the shy pessimist usually trumps. You may be the opposite, leading with a personable part that generally overrides your pessimist, so you're considered an extrovert. From this perspective, any categorization of personality styles, whether the enneagram, the DSM-IV manual of psychiatric diagnoses, the Myers/Briggs, or others, is a description of the ways people's parts have organized.

In the IFS map, the protected parts are called *exiles* because they are the vulnerable ones that we try to lock up in inner prisons or leave frozen in the past. Two kinds of parts protect exiles and also protect the system from them: *managers* and *firefighters*. We will begin with a discussion of exiles.

Exiles

Think of times in your life when you felt humiliated, grief-stricken, terrified, or abandoned. What have you tried to do with the memories, sensations, and emotions from those events? If you are like most people, you have tried to forget about them—to bury them deep in your mind. Think also about what the people around you told you to do with them. As Americans, we grew up in one of the most competitive cultures in the world. Living in it, we've absorbed a great deal of disdain for weakness and impatience with emotional pain. Most of us received some version of the message "Just put it behind you—let it go" from well-meaning family and friends. So we try to exile the fallout from dreadful episodes in the past. But in doing that, we're not only exiling memories, sensations, and emotions; we're also exiling the parts of us that were hurt most by those events. These are often our most sensitive, innocent, open, and intimacy-seeking parts, which contain qualities such as liveliness, playfulness, spontaneity, creativity, and joie de vivre. Because these parts were so sensitive and open, they felt the impact of our traumas the most and were stuck carrying the memories, sensations, and emotions of those events. They are childlike, and like traumatized children, they are changed by the incidents. Rather than help them heal, we add insult to injury. As if they were damaged children in our family who disrupt our household, require a great deal of expense and attention, or embarrass us, we attempt to leave them in the place where they were hurt and move on. When we find that they keep catching up to us, we lock them permanently in the basement and do our best to forget about them.

It's not just the traumatized parts of us that we exile. Think about what it was like to grow up in your family. How much did parts of you disrupt the household or embarrass your parents? What were the unspoken rules in your family about liveliness and spontaneity, anger or assertiveness, sadness or fear, independence and autonomy? How much was your family dominated by parts that wanted to look good to the outside world and needed you to conform to a certain image? How about your peers—how did they treat anyone who acted in ways that weren't cool? In other words, how much trouble did certain parts of you get you into, and what did you try to do with those parts?

In addition to being competitive and intolerant of flaws, Americans tend to be highly image conscious and critical of those who look or act different. Many people in our culture can't deal with any but the most upbeat of emotions, so we are trained to exile any negative ones. The power of positive thinking prevails, but at what cost? What parts were present when you were young that you have exiled in the service of being accepted, "successful," and positive? Author Debbie Ford (1998) writes about messages she received in her family:

> Most of us were raised to believe that people have good qualities and bad qualities. And in order to be accepted we had to get rid of our bad qualities, or at least hide them . . .

I was told, don't be angry, don't be selfish, don't be mean, don't be greedy. "Don't be" was the message I internalized. I started to believe that I was a bad person because sometimes I was mean and sometimes I got angry and sometimes I wanted all the cookies. I believed that to survive in my family and in the world I would have to get rid of these impulses. So I did. Slowly I shoved them so far back into my consciousness that I forgot they were there at all. . . . By the time I was a teenager, I had shut down so much of myself that I was a walking time bomb. (pp. 4, 14)

When you think about it this way, it's disturbing to realize how many wonderful resources and qualities you have cut yourself off from and how limited your life is as a result. But it's important to remember that from the perspective of Western psychology, exiling makes perfect sense. If you only have one mind and you are plagued by troublesome thoughts or emotions, why not try to get rid of them? If thinking about something tragic upsets you, why not train yourself not to think about it and instead to think about something that makes you feel good? That would be the way to go if it worked, and in a limited way it *can* work, at least for a while.

But it only works if you don't mind doing violence to your psyche and becoming less whole as a person. Actually, most of us don't mind because we don't know any better. We feel okay most of the time and we're surviving life. We're doing as well as most people around us. Maybe we have physical or emotional symptoms, but we never connect those to the energy it takes to suppress large portions of our mind.

Fear of exiles

The irony is that once you start the exiling process, it reinforces itself. After they are locked away, those exiles can endanger your system or at least impair your ability to function. So you become even more committed to not going there and to keeping them at bay. After one of my clients, who had been severely sexually abused as a child, got to know one of her exiles, she described the way it felt:

> She craves to recoil, to hide, yet can't chance the slightest of movements. Any sense of being alive would only encourage him [the abuser] to take more. And so she stands erect, the outer trappings of a vacant corpse. Yet her insides are swelled with the onslaught of guilt and growing shame which has claimed every pore, with each cell imploding as with uncontrollable black, raw sewage.

Who would want to re-experience what that little girl felt? When it seems as if the alternatives are to be overwhelmed by that kind of emotion or to keep it locked up, it's no surprise that we have so many exiles.

There are other reasons as well to fear our exiles. They make us feel and act in ways that people disdain or take advantage of—they make us vulnerable, weak, needy, sad, withdrawn, and ashamed. Some of them are so desperate for love that they will steer us toward, or keep us in, hurtful relationships just to get a little affection.

For men, vulnerability means instant humiliation. In our culture, being a man means being able to quickly cut off from hurt feelings without a whimper. In a study of college students, researchers found that when females disclosed feeling depressed to their roommates, they received nurturance. But in response to the same kind of disclosure, the roommates of men were isolating or hostile. It seems that, at least for men, the fear of looking vulnerable is well founded. Remember Thoreau's famous quote, "The mass of men lead lives of quiet desperation." It's no wonder that men keep their desperation quiet. As family therapist Terrence Real (1997) observes:

> Boys and men are granted privilege and special status, but only on the condition that they turn their backs on vulnerability and connection to join the fray. Those who resist, like unconventional men or gay men, are punished for it. Those who lose or who cannot compete, like boys and men with disabilities, or of the wrong class or color, are marginalized, rendered all but invisible. . . . boys and men live each day with a kind of fear that can only rarely be assuaged. Straight is the gait and narrow is the path. One false step and it's a long drop down. If a man is not a winner, he is a loser. And the cost of losing is more than just the game at hand; it is abandonment. (p. 180)

The lonely, stoic prison in which men live is illustrated in the following dialogue between a journalist investigating the brutal murder of Matthew Shepard—the man who in 1998 was bludgeoned beyond recognition in Wyoming just because he was gay—and a friend of the killers:

"If you're telling your feelings, you're kind of a wuss." Brent Jones, a heterosexual man who went to high school with McKinney and Henderson [the murderers], was guiding me through the psychic terrain of a boy's life.

"So what do you do when things hurt?"

"That's why God created whiskey, don't you think? You get drunker than a pig and hope it drains away—or you go home and cry."

"Is that true for most guys, do you think?"

"Yeah, pretty much."

"So secretly you're all wusses, and you know you're wusses, but you can't let anyone know, even though you all know you know."

"You could say that."

"Can you talk to girls about this stuff?"

"Unless you know this is the one—like, you're going to get married, and then you're in so deep you can't help yourself—but if not, if you think she might break up with you, then no, because she might tell someone, and then it gets around, and then everyone thinks you're a wuss. And you don't want people to think you're a wuss, unless you are a wuss, and then you know you're a wuss, and then it doesn't matter." (Wypijewski, 1999, pp. 61–62)

As illustrated in the college roommate study, I believe our culture forces men more than women to exile their vulnerable parts. Women are socialized to exile other parts, like their assertiveness or power, but in some socioeconomic circles that seems to be changing. Women, however, are more likely to be traumatized by sexual assault, abuse, or harassment, and also to have collected burdens of worthlessness from the still-pervasive culture of sexism we swim in.

So we have many good reasons to fear exiles. They can pull us into black holes of emotion or memory, interfere with our functioning, draw us toward or keep us attached to hurtful people, and get us rejected or humiliated by people who disdain vulnerability. There would be no point in going toward them if they were to stay the way they are. Fortunately, however, releasing them from exile is part of a process that transforms them into their original vital states, so it is well worth the effort. But most people have little trust in that possibility, so it's a hard sell. You are being asked to go toward your pain, which runs counter to the way you've lived your whole life. Some clients describe getting close to exiles as the most difficult and scary thing they've ever done. In *The Drama of the Gifted Child* (1994), Swiss psychiatrist Alice Miller provides an example in her description of finally meeting one of her exiles:

> The child within me . . . appeared . . . late in life, wanting to tell me her secret. She approached very hesitantly, speaking first to me in an inarticulate way, but she took me by the hand and led me into territory I had been avoiding all my life because it frightened me. Yet I had to go there; I could not keep on turning my back, for it was my territory, my very own. It was the place I had attempted to forget so many years ago, the same place where I had abandoned the child I once was. There she had to stay, alone with her knowledge, waiting until someone

would come at last to listen to her and believe her. Now I was standing at an open door, ill-prepared, filled with an adult's fear of the darkness and menace of the past, but I could not bring myself to close the door and leave the child alone again until my death. Instead, I made a decision that was to change my life profoundly; to let the child lead me, to put my trust in this nearly autistic being who had survived the isolation of decades. (pp. 24–25)

Sometimes this work takes great courage. You are going toward what you have spent your life avoiding. On the journey, you are likely to encounter a great deal of resistance from the parts of you that have tried so hard to prevent the very thing you are heading toward.

Worthlessness and survival fear

Children are born with a strong need for approval. There are good reasons for this. For much of our species' existence, most children didn't survive infancy due to illness or labor complications, as well as neglect or abuse. Even now, thirty million children die each year before age five. Human infants are high-maintenance organisms. They require constant attention and effort, remaining dependent on caregivers for an extraordinary period relative to other animals. Today, in many parts of the world, if a family's resources are limited, a young child's survival will depend on how much the parents value him or her. Disapproval can equal death.

Consequently, children are born with an overriding desire to be valued and an intense terror when they sense they aren't. What people call self-esteem is really a sense of security that one was valued as a child and is likely to survive. If caregivers seem to like you, you might make it; if not, you may be doomed.

These early survival fears abate when a child receives consistent messages about his or her worth and the safety of the environment. A well-nurtured child can ease into the world as if stepping into a warm bath. The parts of the child's personality designed to ensure survival relax and allow the child access to a rich inner life filled with wonderful sensations and resources. The more a child is able to intuit this inner realm, the more secure the child feels because, in addition to sensing creative, adventurous, and playful parts, he or she will sense the Self—who he or she really is behind all the fear. As described earlier, the awareness of our soul-like Self provides transcendent grace—a spontaneous sense of connection to something greater and a knowledge that we are loved from within.

A field within psychology called *attachment theory* has produced an impressive body of research demonstrating the power of our early interactions with caregivers over our lifelong belief systems and sense of emotional security. According to this theory, the nature of the attachments we formed to our parents can determine how we are in intimate relationships throughout the rest of our lives. From my perspective, this is because parts of us take to heart any message from a caregiver that we're not valued and, thereafter, carry a sense of worthlessness and the survival terror that accompanies it.

There are many ways in our culture to get the message that we are worthless. Overt abuse and neglect are the two most obvious ways that children are given this message, but many others exist as well. For example, many parents discover that making children think they're not worth much can be motivating. People will be extraordinarily compliant and hard working when they think their lives are at stake.

Many of my highly successful adult clients were fed a constant diet of shame as children or, at best, were deliberately made to worry about their value. Many men, for example, report that their father never told them directly that he loved them and gave them many reasons to question his love. It's not uncommon for me to hear stories of fathers who believed that showing unconditional love would spoil their children, making them soft or complacent. Some of these sons became so dominated by the desire to please that they work incessantly and sacrifice all other aspects of their lives to demonstrate their worth to parents and society.

At the same time, families are delicately balanced ecologies, and it is almost impossible for parents to avoid inadvertently giving their kids that unloved message from time to time. A sibling is born who suddenly sucks all your parents' attention from you, and you're too young to understand why. Your father is about to lose his job and explodes at you over something small. If parents have the time and space to recognize when they have dumped a burden of worthlessness onto a child, they can repair the damage with an apology or a hug, but, especially in today's frenetic world, it's hard to always be that aware. Consequently, most of us have emerged from our families with sizable burdens of worthlessness and then accumulate even more from our society.

Win or be a loser

In the United States, we learn to compete from preschool on. We have to win to avoid being a loser, which is about the worst insult that exists in our culture. I recently saw a cartoon in which a father is kneeling down with his arm around his young son's shoulders and saying, "Just remember, son, it doesn't matter whether you win or lose—unless you want Daddy's love." That father is only saying out loud what many parents think, because they are so afraid themselves of being losers. Beliefs such as "I am worth something only to the extent that I beat others at a test, game, or promotion, or have more money, popularity, beauty, or things than my peers" become so internalized that we have little awareness of how often we think them. Even with friends, parts of us constantly compare our status with theirs, secretly envying their triumphs and cheering their failures—always keeping score. We respect our friends only as long as other people think they're cool.

To give a personal example, as an early adolescent I was very self-conscious and insecure about my appearance and status. I was short, had braces and acne, and my nose had suddenly exploded to the point of dominating my face in the way that it does when some kids hit puberty. It didn't help that I was the only Jew in a peer group of Christians who would commonly make jokes about Jews, remember I was there, and then say, "Oh, sorry, Schwartz." I was desperate to be popular and tried hard to fit in with the cool group of boys, but their way of relating was to put each other down. It was a kind of dominance game where if you could parry with them, you were accepted, but if they ever smelled blood, you became the target of a sadistic verbal attack. I was too easily hurt to keep up and, despite absorbing deep emotional bruises, kept coming back for more. I hated the parts of me that would feel injured and tried to exile them so I could "take it" like the other boys could. Exiles are often victims of this kind of double or triple whammy. They are hurt by the initial trauma, then attacked by our protective parts for being weak, and finally given life sentences and locked in inner dungeons.

Fortunately, I withdrew from that group before my sensitive parts became permanent exiles, but I was left with a strong fear of opening up to males enough to develop close friendships. I felt the way Woody Allen once did when he said he felt like a hemophiliac in a razor blade factory—everyone had the potential to start a bleed I couldn't stop. Consequently, I went through a long, friendless period during which I constantly felt like a loser of monumental proportions but pretended to family and peers that things were fine.

That sense of being a loser has plagued me throughout my life, floating up from the depths of my psyche whenever there's a dry period in my social life. I've worked with so many clients who were similarly scarred by the competitive popularity contests American society has become to have concluded that most Americans walk around believing deep down that they are losers. We spend our lives terrified that someone will see that we are while trying to prove to ourselves and everyone else that we aren't.

The drive for redemption

The parts of us that feel like losers and that think we are worthless constitute for many people their most dreaded set of exiles. One reason is that those parts are desperate for redemption. They become obsessed with getting the person who gave them the message of worthlessless to reverse that message. This is why many people become dysfunctionally attached to an abusive parent or to someone who looks, sounds, or acts like that parent. They become addicted to any fleeting moments of approval and put up with mountains of denigration and exploitation just to get it.

As high as our exiles soar when given the message that they are loved, they crash equally hard when the perceived redeemer withdraws that love. It is as if each of us walks around with an invisible bear trap on our leg, searching desperately for the person who holds the key to unlock it. Our exiles believe the key holder is the person who put the trap there in the first place or a replica of that person. Unfortunately, usually such a person also carries more bear traps—a fact that we ignore in our haste to be released from the pain. Consequently, our exiles lead us to someone who at times can make us feel great, but who at other times applies more bear traps to our legs, making us all the more desperate. This is how we become addicted to people who hurt us. Our exiles so long for the hit of love or approval from a designated redeemer that they are willing to suffer (and sometimes believe they deserve) the abuse that accompanies it.

For many of us, the survival terror and sense of worthlessness that certain exiles carry become the governing forces in our lives, organizing our choice of partners and our consuming drive to achieve or accumulate. The longing and hope in these parts are so powerful that even from their dungeon cells, they have a special unconscious influence over our decisions. We live in fear of any event that triggers that sense of being a loser, yet like a moth to a flame, we're constantly drawn toward people or events that might release us from that curse. Those parts are okay as long as hope for redemption is on the horizon. When something happens to extinguish that hope, watch out!

On some dreaded occasions, the tinderbox of emotion

that our exiles carry is ignited. It turns out that our underground pools of pain and shame are combustible, as if they were filled with gasoline. Certain events or interactions act like a match, igniting flames of emotion that threaten to consume us. We re-experience the burdens of terror, loneliness, humiliation, abandonment, despair, or worthlessness that our exiles have been carrying for us. If those exiles fully take over, we can become incapacitated. Obsessed and regressed, unable to sleep or concentrate, constantly agitated or depressed, we invite psychiatric diagnosis. We can't work and sometimes can't get out of bed. This is the worst nightmare of our protective parts. This is why they spend so much energy trying to keep our exiles exiled and our environment free of events or people that might trigger them. This is why our protective parts build fortresses around us. This dark, fiery night of the soul can motivate us to try to find new ways to lock up our exiles—to patch the cracks in our fortress and find new distractions. Or, if we have courage and help, fortress-shattering events can lead us to a rebirth through the healing of our exiles.

Managers

I call the protective parts that are responsible for our day-to-day safety the managers. For many of us, they are the voices we hear most often, to the point where we come to think of ourselves as those voices or thoughts. While we rely on their opinions, strategies, and judgments, we also feel constrained by or annoyed with them.

Managers are the parts of you that want to control everything. They try to control your relationships and environment so you're never in a position to be humiliated, abandoned, rejected, attacked, or anything else unexpected and hurtful. They try to control your appearance, performance, emotions, and thoughts for the same reason. In this protective effort, they often have a "never again" philosophy, like the Jews and the Holocaust: "Never again will I let you be so weak, needy, dependent, open, trusting, happy, risk taking . . ." and so on.

Managers are the parts that monitor how you're coming across to parents, bosses, and others you depend on. They scan for cracks in your masks of invulnerability, friendliness, and perfection, and compare you unfavorably to cultural icons or to the Joneses next door or in the next office. Managers interpret the world to you and create the narratives you live by. They are authors and enforcers of the story you have about yourself that is called your identity. They create stories like, "I'm a nice person," "I'm a hard worker," and "I'm very strong" based on feedback from the outside world as well as to serve their protective purposes. That is, a habitually nice person exiles angry parts, a hard worker doesn't give much time to playful or intimacy-loving parts, and a strong person keeps vulnerable parts hidden. Managers create negative narratives for similarly protective reasons. If you believe you're basically unlovable or a loser, you won't take many risks and won't be disappointed. Likewise, they can control you with the stories they tell you about the outside world, such as "Men are dangerous" or "Life isn't supposed to be fun." Managers are your reality makers. It's likely that you are so identified with some managers that you've lived your entire life without questioning these stories about yourself and the world. It's no wonder you only have fleeting glimpses of who you really are.

Many of the stories managers tell us about ourselves come

from our family or culture. Managers are the internalizers of our system—they open the door of our psyche and welcome in the values that surround us. They believe our survival depends on the mercy of the outside world, so they take on the voices of authority in an effort to get us to behave appropriately. For example, if you were to focus on your inner critic, you might find that it carries the voice, image, or words of one of your parents berating you for not trying hard enough or looking right. This part also evaluates you based on cultural standards of beauty and achievement, and constantly points out areas in which you don't measure up. In this way, your managers suck in the emotions and beliefs of significant others and the culture at large. They are what some psychotherapies call your "false self" and what some spiritual traditions refer to as your "ego that keeps you attached to the world." But, again, it's a mistake to think they are, at their root, the way they seem. They may use the voice or image of a parent in order to have more influence, but that's a mask or prop—not who they really are.

The best way to understand managers is to think of them as striving to preempt anything that might touch our exiles. They want to protect our exiles, but they also disdain them for being weak or needy. Managers blame those vulnerable parts for getting us hurt. They have tremendous fear of being overwhelmed by exiled pain or shame. Like sentries, they're always on guard for events that might trigger exiles and are always strategizing ways to avoid such events. They want to change the world to make it more predictable and less threatening, and they fear the consequences of relinquishing any of their power. If your mind were a government, managers would be the right-wing coalition that was trying to maintain law and order domestically and whose foreign policy was based on either dominating or retreating from the world. For many of us, they rule like a military junta, oppressing much of the rest of the population and constantly fearing a coup.

We often resent our managers because we experience them as the constant inner chatter that keeps us from concentrating, the self-hating voices that never let up, the fear that holds us back in relationships, the impulse to do for others that makes us neglect ourselves, the drive for achievement that consumes all our energy, the feeling of victimhood that others tire of, the sense of entitlement that makes us inconsiderate, and so on. Managers form the layer of noise the gods placed in us to make it hard to learn the secret of happiness. Yet when we get to know them, we find that they are generally much younger than they first appear and are overburdened with responsibility and fear. Like parentified children, they are in over their heads and, consequently, have become rigid and punitive. They often feel unappreciated and hate their jobs but think that somebody has to do it. I have a great deal of compassion and respect for your managers and hope you can, too.

Across people, I've found that there are common manager roles. Below I present several of the most common. Let's begin with our longtime companions: the critics.

Critics: taskmasters and approval seekers

You are probably so used to the constant stream of inner evaluation of self and others that, like a music soundtrack to your life, it becomes background noise. When you first focus on that noise, it's often startling to realize how much of it you do. If you did focus on it, you might notice that there were several different parts you could differentiate, based on their motives. That is, some are taskmasters that feel responsible for making you work hard and that have high, often unreachable, standards of performance. They frequently compare you unfavorably to those around you or in the media and blast you for any mistakes. They use the same measuring stick and tactics to motivate others as well.

Other critics carry the responsibility for getting social approval and are focused on your appearance and the way you behave with others. They have you in front of the mirror or on the bathroom scale all the time, highlighting all your body's flaws. They monitor how popular you are and do their own form of comparing to those around you. They are also constantly evaluating the appearance and popularity of others.

Because they have different responsibilities and agendas for protecting you, taskmasters and approval seekers are often in conflict. One wants you to move ahead ruthlessly, work constantly, and let people know how much they disappoint you. The other wants you to be nice to everyone so they'll like you, never threaten anyone with your performance, and spend your time socializing so you are sure to have friends. This example brings up the concept of polarization again. There are as many natural polarizations among protective parts over the best way to run a person as there are among politicians over how to run a country. Both of these critics are often polarized with a different manager: the pessimist.

Pessimist

When you think about taking a risk, what happens inside your mind? If you're like me, immediately a voice (sometimes a chorus) of doom and gloom hijacks the inner microphone and tries to talk you out of it. My voice is often accompanied by a strong lethargy and apathy. The second I begin entertaining a vision of change, in the words of writer Gregg Levoy (1997), it's as if ". . . a horde of caveats and commandments latch onto [the vision] like antibodies on an invading bacteria" (p. 219). If I persist toward the risk, my pessimist quickly turns into a critic, trying to undermine my confidence by spotlighting my faults and reminding me of all the times I've failed or been rejected in the past. Writer Anne Lamott (1999) knows her pessimist and calls it "Bad Mind." When her car broke down in traffic, she wrote:

> It was a nightmare: Bad Mind kicked in. Bad Mind can't wait for this kind of opportunity: "I told you so," Bad Mind says. It whispers to me that I am doomed because I'm such a loser. Bad Mind can lean ever so slightly toward paranoia. "The woman you bought this car from," it whispered, "is already on a plane back to Iran, celebrating." (p. 109)

Pessimists are often targets for our hate because they are the obvious obstacles on our path toward success and happiness. It's easy to miss their protective nature. If Lamott were to focus on Bad Mind with compassion and ask it questions, she would find that it's nothing like what she thought. Having had innumerable conversations with my own and my clients' pessimists, I expect her inner dialogue might go something like this:

LAMOTT: Why are you always calling me names and making me feel bad?

BAD MIND: Because you are a loser—you make so many mistakes, and bad things are always happening to you.

LAMOTT: Yeah, I screw up sometimes. Maybe I should have shopped longer before I bought that car. But it doesn't help for you to rub it in all the time. What are you afraid would happen if you didn't?

BAD MIND: If I didn't, you'd screw up even more. And you'd keep getting disappointed.

LAMOTT: So you're trying to protect me from disappointment?

BAD MIND: That's right. You do so many reckless things, and you keep getting hurt.

LAMOTT: Where did you get the idea I was such a loser?

BAD MIND: From Mom, who called you lazy, and from the boys who rejected you in junior high.

Many people diagnosed as depressed are dominated by their pessimist. If it decides it has to shut you down to keep you from getting hurt, it can make you feel totally apathetic, listless, hopeless, and worthless. In that role, it is effective not only in paralyzing you but also in keeping a lid on the rawer, more acute emotions of your exiles.

Caregiver

While our culture socializes men to be dominated by striving, autonomous, and entitled managers, many women are still taught to lead with their caregivers. These are the parts that take responsibility for the well-being of everyone around you, putting their welfare high above yours on your internal list of priorities.

They worry constantly about how others are doing, take on more than your share of the workload, sacrifice your leisure time to care for others, and make people dependent on you. They often carry the belief that others are more valuable than you and that if you don't do for everyone, no one will like you. Caregiver parts tend to create relationships in which your partner or children depend on you but also exploit you and don't respect you.

Victim

I have found in my clients and myself a part that can distort and amplify any slight to the point where we feel totally victimized and deserving of extreme forms of compensation. When my wife used to hurt my feelings, this part would take over and demand that she not only apologize but also listen to every detail of how she hurt me and promise never to do anything like that again. My wife's hurtful action would be entered into this part's register of all the other things she and other people had done to me, and I would frequently remind myself and her of those things. This victim part could also excuse hurtful things I might do, saying that I had to because of what had happened to me, and could make me feel entitled to more resources or less work as compensation. It is this victim part that people complain about when they say scornfully, "You're just feeling sorry for yourself." Unfortunately, that message has permeated our culture to the point that it interferes with our ability to have compassion for any of our parts.

Self-imitating part

When working with clients, I've found many times that through the IFS process, they shift into a state that seems to embody many qualities of the Self, but the work doesn't flow. They seem to be curious and care about their parts or their partner, yet if I listen carefully, I can detect a subtle hidden agenda behind their words or actions. For example, in a couples session, a wife was very upset with her husband, and he seemed quite reasonable and receptive to what she was saying such that it appeared that he was in his Self and she was in a victim part. As I paid closer attention to his tone and words, however, I noticed a hollow compliance, protective distance, and slight condescension. In other words, while he seemed to be caring, his heart wasn't open, and he was using this reasonable part to keep up an image of being the "together" one. When I worked with his internal world, this same Self-imitating part would interact with his other parts, and I was confused as to why they didn't respond the way most people's parts do in the presence of Self. It took me some time to identify the part as a Self-imitating part (rather than his Self) because I have one that I was closely identified with.

Because it seems so similar to Self, for many people a Self-imitating part is the most difficult protector to detect. The only way I can detect this part in myself is to check to see how open my heart is or to notice if I have an agenda while I interact with someone.

There are many other typical managers, and you may find some that are unique to you. Because managers can be so constraining, we often have a love/hate relationship with them, as we might with a dominating parent, boss, or spouse. We hate how much some criticize us or how others keep us frozen and self-conscious. We would love to get rid of them and feel free at last. At the same time, we feel dependent on their direction and protection. For many of us, those managers have always been there, so the prospect of life without all the chatter and inner tension seems strange and threatening. "If I didn't call myself lazy and stupid, I might not try so hard." "If I didn't take care of everyone else before myself, maybe no one would like me." "If I let people see who I really was, they'd reject me." Those parts have gotten us this far, so why take a chance? In addition, if all the inner noise or outer activity died down, we might be pulled into our exiles' desperate world.

To relate effectively to managers, it's important to appreciate the responsibilities they carry, the constant stress they're under, and the sacrifices they've made to protect us. Misunderstanding the nature of parts has been one of the biggest sources of human suffering. Because some managers do things that get in the way of our full enjoyment of life, we fight with them and curse their existence. Well-meaning therapists of every ilk encourage us to stand up to inner bullies, cast aside "codependent" caregiver voices, rebel against the impulse toward perfection, steamroll over fearful pessimists, and exorcise inner bigots. They give us affirmations to counter inner critics and interpretations to correct their irrational beliefs.

Fighting against constraining managers makes common sense and would be the way to go if it worked. But it doesn't because it's based on a faulty premise: that parts are the roles they're in—that the books are their covers. When you get to know them, you find that most managers hate their roles and are much more than their roles. I have never found a part that was purely evil or destructive, and I've worked with sex offenders and other people who did evil things. Emerson said, "And what is a weed? A plant whose virtues have not been discovered." When our parts seem like weeds to be pulled, it's because we haven't taken the time to learn of their beauty. Poet Rainer Maria Rilke (1984) knew about this when he counseled a younger poet who was oppressed by self-critical doubt that if he stopped fighting it, ". . . the day will come when instead of being a destroyer, it will become one of your best workers—perhaps the most intelligent of all the ones that are building your life" (p. 102).

Some managers are plagued by the opposite problem: we like them too much. Like parentified children, we overload them with responsibility and power. I have worked with many men, for example, who depended on their intellectual, problem-solving parts to guide all their decisions. These parts seemed to rationally weigh all the data, but their ultimate choices usually favored the safe and narrow path over any that involved intimacy or emotion. Our culture prizes and rewards these internal Mr. Spocks because they can build suspension bridges and Internet businesses, so we come to rely increasingly on them. We let those parts put distance between us and our more adventurous, intimacy-loving, and juicy feelings.

The point to stress in this discussion of managers is that they are doing their best to keep us safe and, for most of us, that has not been an easy job. We come into a world filled with real dangers—disease, poverty, crime, discrimination, oppression—and, depending on our family's and culture's history, we inherit additional fears. Throughout our childhoods, we experience varying degrees of rejection, abandonment, betrayal, and humiliation. All these influences lead us to lose trust in our natural, internal leadership—our Self. Managers took over at scary or traumatic times in our past and committed never to allow anything like that to happen again. They saw how hard it was to survive in the world and decided to shape us into the most acceptable form possible. They realized how devastating the emotions carried by our exiles can be and pledged to keep us safe. In a way, they sacrificed their enjoyment of life to protect the rest of our system.

Firefighters

As hard as our managers work to construct a protective fortress around us and to control us, our relationships, and events in the world, the world has a way of breaking through their defenses at times and triggering our exiles. For all the reasons discussed earlier, this is a very threatening state. It can feel like the panic of a red alert in a nuclear reactor—as though we're about to have a meltdown. We all have parts that go into action at that point to put out the fire, so I call them firefighters. This might seem like an odd term for this group of parts because in some ways they are more like fire setters that create crises in our lives. But I call them firefighters because that maintains a focus on the protective nature of even the destructive things they do. Firefighters do whatever it takes to deliver us out of the red-alert condition.

What's your first impulse when you begin to feel the desperate burning of hurt, emptiness, worthlessness, shame, rejection, loneliness, or fear? Which urge do you act upon to take away that fire in your belly? Which ones do you only fantasize? Many of us, in a compromise with our managers, binge on something socially acceptable—work, food, exercise, television, shopping, dieting, flirting, sleeping, prescription drugs, cigarettes, coffee, daydreams and fantasies, gambling, meditating, or thrill-seeking activities—in an effort to distract from the flames until they burn themselves out or are doused. When our effort doesn't work, our firefighters will resort to more drastic and less acceptable means, such as illegal drugs, alcohol, suicidal thoughts or behavior, rage and acts of domination, self-mutilation, compulsive sexual activity, secret affairs, stealing, or getting into punitive relationships. Many of my clients resort to the second list immediately because their firefighters have found over the years that the first list doesn't do much to snuff the flames of emotion. Firefighters will use virtually any thought, activity, or substance if it works.

For some people, firefighters use the body. Sudden pains or illnesses can be effective distractions. Firefighters can amplify physical pain or disease that already exists, lower resistance to viruses or bacteria, or push physiological buttons that trigger genetic conditions. From this perspective, the dualistic notion that it's either in your head or it's biochemical uselessly dichotomizes a deeply interwoven relationship between body and mind. Our parts profoundly affect our physiology and vice versa. How we treat our bodies—what we ingest and how much we sleep, exercise, work, dance, get massaged, and meditate—strongly affects how calm or upset different parts are.

Another set of firefighters favors the impulsive retreat. If they sense an impending rejection, they make us run or push the potential rejector away. We're often unconscious of their work, aware only of an impulse to get away or to lash out. These firefighters can make us want to suddenly bolt from a room in a threatening situation or get sleepy, confused, dizzy, or numb. I've had clients who, as we approached exiles, suddenly fell totally asleep, became mindlessly blank, or experienced vertigo.

The image I often have of a firefighter is of a teenaged boy or girl who is responsible for an infant who's screaming, and nothing the teen does seems to help. The babysitter will try to stick something in the infant's mouth to calm it down (for example, food, drugs, or alcohol), will desperately try to find someone else to take care of it (flirting or affairs), or will find a distraction for itself and everyone else until the infant stops crying (television, meditating, or shopping). If none of these efforts work, the frustrated adolescent is likely to throw the baby into a closet to drown out its wails and hope it will go to sleep. This image conveys the compassion I've come to feel for your firefighters. They have dreadful jobs and are often hated and attacked by your managers as well as by the people around you.

So your managers and firefighters are both trying to protect your system, but they do so in opposite ways. Managers are preemptive—they try to anticipate anything that might upset your exiles and try to control your environment to keep you safe. Most managers are also concerned about pleasing people. Firefighters are reactive—they frantically jump into action as soon as the exiles are upset and the fire starts. Their urgency makes them impulsively unconcerned about consequences. They often make you feel out of control, and they frequently displease people. They're the parts that can make you fat, addicted, hostile, sneaky, sick, insensitive, and compulsive. They're the ones about whom the apostle Paul was talking when he said, "I don't understand what I do; for I don't do what I would like to do but instead I do what I hate" (Romans, 7:15). As was true for Paul, managers often hate firefighters despite the fact that, just like managers, firefighters are trying to protect us—just in a different way. In turn, firefighters often rebel against the shame that managers heap on them by increasing the destructiveness of their activities.

It's very difficult for most people to believe that destructive impulses come from good parts in bad roles. I've worked with many seemingly evil parts in clients who were sex offenders, conduct-disordered kids, and sexual abuse survivors—parts that said they were the devil, wanted to kill me, had molested little girls, randomly attacked people on the street, or recreated past abuse inside the person's life. All of these parts had similar stories to tell. All of them were good parts in bad roles. Some were heroes, in an odd way. The reason they carried so much rage or sexual energy was because they had taken the bullet for the rest of the system when the person had been abused. Like Secret Service agents jumping in front of the president to shield him from an assassin, they had sacrificed themselves and protected my client by staying present for the abuse while other parts were allowed to check out. Consequently, they absorbed toxic amounts of the abuser's energy. That energy drove them to act in ways they themselves didn't like. I have worked with sex offenders enough to know of the exiled pain and shame they carry from childhoods of abuse, neglect, and loss. Wordsworth said, "If we could read the secret history of our enemies, we should find in each man's life sorrow and suffering enough to disarm all hostility."

When firefighters take over, they can make us feel as if we're possessed by something out of our control, so they make easy targets of demonization. Thus start endless inner vicious cycles mirroring the one between God and Satan. We render a part evil and try to get rid of it. Like a child being ostracized from a family, it feels hurt, ashamed, and angry. As a result, it becomes more extreme and rebellious, and tries harder to take over. The righteous managers try harder to eliminate it. After several rounds of feeling attacked, some firefighters, like some kids, do have fantasies of destroying the rest of the system and can become dangerous. My experience, however, is that if the cycle is reversed and they are treated with respect and compassion, even those firefighters apparently bent on evil quickly drop their destructive masks.

It's important to remember, however, that no matter how compassionately you treat your firefighters, they won't be able to change as long as there's a fire to be fought. In other words, until the exiles that they protect or distract you from are healed, your firefighters will still have the same old impulses. Also keep in mind that not all firefighters are as destructive or extreme as those discussed above. Some of mine include parts that make me work all the time, feel hungry for sugar or fat, and yearn for a mindless distraction. Because these firefighters are pervasive and normalized in our culture, I hardly notice their presence until I find myself in front of the computer, refrigerator, or TV. When you stop to think about it, a huge segment of the U.S. economy is based on providing activities, substances, and goods designed to help our firefighters do their distracting and numbing. They help us avoid awareness of the pain in our country and in our selves. If all Americans healed their exiles, the stock market might tumble, but we would not put up with the kinds of imbalances that exist in this country nor with politicians who exacerbate those imbalances.

No More Firefighters, Managers, and Exiles

So firefighters take us far away from our present-centered, embodied state of Self. The good news, however, is that once released from their extreme roles, firefighters often transform into our most lively, joyful, and resilient parts. They become passionately engaged in life and can be powerful motivators. Think of what your life might be like if all the energy you spent, for example, angrily stewing about what others have done to you, or obsessively daydreaming about your missing soulmate, were available to you in the present moment and were channeled toward fully enjoying whatever you are doing now. What if the strength of your urge to binge became a confidence and focus that helped you connect with people? As hard as it may be to believe, such transformations are possible because these parts are much more than the roles they have been forced into.

These three groups of parts' roles (exiles, managers, and firefighters) exist because of all the pain and shame you accrued in your life and the ways you were taught to relate to that pain and shame. Since you didn't learn how to heal that pain and shame, you had to exile it, which led to the need for all these protectors. These three groups are polarized such that when one takes over, it tries to dominate your experience for fear that if it gives you access to other parts, you'll do or think something dangerous. When your internal system functions in this way, your experience of the world is impoverished. For example, many people dominated by managers live bland lives spent planning their safety. Those hijacked by firefighters have minds in constant agitation as they move from one distraction to another, never slowing down for fear of their exiles catching up. Those whose exiles have taken over are constantly in acute and seemingly regressed states of fear, sadness, or shame. Anyone dominated by a single group of parts exhibits a rigidity and narrowness because only a small, extreme portion of them is present.

As you access and use the innate healing resources of your Self, gradually you find that you no longer have managers, exiles, and firefighters. Not that your parts disappear—they just transform into roles they prefer. As that happens, you feel more integrated and solid, but with a wide range of emotion and expression. When life becomes stormy, you sense the deep peace of your Self that lies beneath the waves your parts are riding. You can be the "I" in the storm and, from that centered place, can calm your parts and the people around you. Because your parts no longer carry burdens of fear, shame, rage, despair, and so on, they get along with one another, trust the leadership of your Self, and are in roles they enjoy. They become your allies and advisors, lending different perspectives and passions to your present-centered experience. In that state, things that used to trigger automatic responses in you lose their charge, and you can break lifelong patterns related to work, intimate relationships, your body, creativity, and more.

For example, a client I'll call Brett was dominated by entitled, womanizing firefighters that were constantly scanning for new conquests. He had a long history of becoming infatuated with a woman, losing interest soon after successfully seducing her, and then looking for a replacement. He finally met a woman he really loved, but, despite his best intentions, he found himself doing the same thing with her. When I asked about his sexual experience, he said that he didn't really enjoy the sex act that much. It was more like a tension release—the thrill was in the hunt. As we talked to the part in charge of this pattern, it revealed that it was afraid if it didn't keep finding new women, he would feel worthless. He suffered from the syndrome Groucho Marx made famous with his line, "I'd never join a club that would have me as a member." Once a woman showed Brett that she liked him, Brett stopped respecting her, figuring that if she liked him, she couldn't be that cool. She no longer assuaged his worthlessness, so his firefighter had to find someone else. After we unloaded the burden of worthlessness from one of Brett's exiles, his firefighter stepped out of its scanning and seducing role and began helping Brett look for adventures in other aspects of his life. He took up photography and traveled to exotic locations with the woman he loved. He reported that his sex life improved because sex was no longer a unidimensional, perfunctory aspect of a larger self-soothing pattern. Now it was a beautiful dance filled with a variety of emotions, from innocent awe to adventurous experimenting. Brett no longer needed his partner to adore him or admire his performance. Instead he enjoyed the many different parts of her that showed up during their lovemaking.

As you might be surmising, the IFS process is about changing people's internal politics. By virtue of growing up in a culture and family dominated by certain qualities and exiling of others, your mind reflects that hierarchical arrangement. Reading this book is a subversive activity. It aims to help you replace your authoritarian inner government with a form of pluralism in which each part feels appreciated, is free to do what it prefers, and trusts the noncoercive, heart-centered leadership of your Self.

Chapter Five

THE IFS CLIENT

This chapter is designed to give people who have decided to work with an IFS therapist a few tips regarding what to expect.

If you are like most people, you will initially be reluctant when your IFS therapist asks if you want to focus inside, both because it's unfamiliar to you and because you may fear what you'll find in there. Your therapist will respect that reluctance and will help you explore it. In IFS, we don't pressure clients to go farther or faster than they feel is safe. Instead, your therapist will ask you about your concerns about going inside and will discuss how those concerns might be handled. Over the years, we have learned specific ways of working that make going inside—even to very emotional places—quite safe, without your feeling overwhelmed. In all the work, our first priority is your safety, and we rely on your feedback to help us know whenever something doesn't feel safe.

When you first begin, you don't know how safe the process is, and you have every right to ask your therapist to spell out exactly how your concerns will be addressed before you let him or her lead you on a journey inward. You also have every right not to go in if you don't find your therapist's reassurances satisfactory or if it doesn't feel like the right time to do it. In other words, **you** are in control of what happens in the therapy. If you feel pressured or sense any other problem with your therapist, don't hesitate to tell him or her. IFS therapists will listen carefully to your feedback and will take it seriously. We know that we are not always as sensitive or aware as we would like to be, and we value your perceptions, which help us become even more attuned to your individual needs.

You may also find that you bristle when your therapist asks about different "parts" of you. Some people have no problem with that language because they already speak it. It's common parlance to say, "A part of me is furious with my partner, but another part thinks I'm wrong" or "A part of me loves to write, but another one is afraid people will laugh at it" or "A part of me is glad to be here, but another part wishes I were still in bed." Parts language is a natural way to express the different things we are thinking or feeling. One reason your IFS therapist asks you to focus inside is to help you recognize that your parts have more to them than you thought. Another reason is that the act of listening to your parts helps them relax.

If, however, you are put off by parts language, just let your therapist know, and he or she will use any term you prefer. Some people want to stay with commonly used words such as *thoughts* and *emotions;* others prefer talking about *aspects* of themselves. The term doesn't matter, and again, **you** are in control.

If you agree to go inside, your therapist will ask you what part you want to explore first. From years of experience, we have found that it's safer to start with some parts than others. This is because human internal systems organize into parts that protect us and other parts that are vulnerable and need to be protected. When you consider focusing on a vulnerable part, you may experience thoughts that tell you not to do that, that wonder if the therapist or process can be trusted, or that try to distract you from that focus. Such thoughts, which come from protective parts, are common and natural. It is your protectors' job to be careful and not let anyone into your system until they trust that it is safe to do so. IFS therapists may encourage you to listen to these protectors by having you focus on those thoughts before you get close to any vulnerable parts. You will be asked to listen inside to the fears of your protectors and then tell your therapist what those fears are. Examples of common protector fears include being judged by the therapist, being overwhelmed by vulnerable parts, not doing it right, not being able to change anything so why bother, and so on. Your IFS therapist will discuss these fears with you to reassure your protectors about how you can proceed safely. You will then ask your protectors if they are satisfied and see if they give permission for you to get in touch with a vulnerable part.

The above passages make it sound as if your therapist has you talking to yourself, and that's sort of true. Have you ever found yourself feeling sad but not knowing why? Then you wait for a time, and the answer comes. The IFS process is like that. When a client does this work, he or she focuses on a thought or feeling, asks a question of it, and waits patiently for an answer to come from inside rather than trying to guess or imagine what the part would say. This may seem strange, and you may think you won't be able to do it, but our experience indicates that after people get over the initial strangeness, they are surprised at their ability to have meaningful inner dialogues.

As they focus inside, some people begin a kind of imagery process in which they can "see" their parts. Many others, however, just hear a vague voice or have a fuzzy sense of a part's presence. The only time people have trouble in IFS therapy is when protective parts of them that are accustomed to being in charge won't allow them to listen to or trust the validity of the voices, images, or impressions that come. If that is the case, your therapist may help you ask the protector about its fear of opening the door to other parts. If no fears emerge and the curtain is still pulled over the work, you and your therapist can do something else for a time and perhaps try again later. Sometimes protective parts need more time before they will let you inside. We respect their pace.

Once you focus on a part and find it (people can often sense where it seems to be located in their body and use that as a focal point), your therapist will ask you how you feel toward it. Because your family and your culture valued some of your parts and feared or disliked others, it is likely that your inner world will reflect that. For example, many people grew up in families in which the direct expression of anger was outlawed, so they had to stifle the assertive part of them that wanted to speak about injustices in the family or wanted them to stand up for themselves. Other parts took on their family's beliefs about anger, so whenever they began to have angry thoughts, they would immediately criticize themselves for having such thoughts or distract themselves. This example represents what IFS calls an inner polarization between two parts. If, as that person, you started to focus on your angry part and your therapist asked how you felt toward it, you would probably say you feared or hated it. When you fear or hate any part, it is hard to have a productive dialogue with it. So when your therapist heard you say that, he or she would have you ask the parts that were making you fear or hate the angry one (or feel any other extreme emotion toward it) if they would be willing to "step back"—to separate their feelings from you for a little while so you could get to know the angry one better.

To make this more concrete, imagine that you are the leader of a group of people who have many conflicts with each other, and your therapist is trying to help you calm them down. Each time you start to talk to one person, another one thinks you're going to side with the first one or give him or her more power. So the second person tries to influence you to dislike and stay away from the first one. With all this vying for your favor, you won't get very far. If, instead, you can talk to each person individually without interference from the others, you can form a trusting alliance with each side, which will facilitate future negotiations. This is why your therapist will frequently ask one part to step back so you can talk to another part.

With some parts, however, you may not believe that it's safe to get close to them at all or without the armoring of protective parts. It is likely that you have some parts you'd just like to get rid of or at least keep locked up inside. For example, most people don't see much value in getting closer to their despair, their brutal inner judge, their terror, their rage, and so on. There wouldn't be any reason to get closer to these parts if they stayed the way they are. One of the big discoveries of IFS, however, is that as you get to know these parts and learn why they are the way they are—that is, as you witness their stories from the past about how they were forced into the roles they are in—they change. It turns out that there aren't any inherently bad parts, just good parts in bad roles—

good parts carrying extreme beliefs or emotions from things that happened in the past. If you focus on them from a nonjudging, curious, or open-hearted perspective, they eventually transform into something valuable. This may seem hard to believe, and it certainly runs counter to the ways our culture and many religions tell us to relate to these parts, but it is confirmed every day in offices of IFS therapists all over the world.

If, in response to your request, a part does step back, you will feel an immediate shift in demeanor, emotion, and perspective. At that point, the therapist is likely to ask you again how you feel toward the original target part. You may notice that you have now shifted into a different extreme state. To stay with the anger example, suppose you first hated and wanted to get rid of your angry part and, when that hate stepped back, suddenly you feel afraid of the anger. If this happens, your therapist will ask your fear to step back as well and will continue asking parts to step back until you begin feeling one of the following toward the original (angry) target part: curious, compassionate, confident, or calm. The therapist won't ask you to conjure up one of those feelings, and you don't have to try to do so; your therapist will just keep asking parts to step back until you spontaneously report such a state.

This spontaneous arising of valuable leadership qualities as parts separate is related to another significant IFS discovery—that we all have those kinds of qualities within us. Your parts carry all the irrational and unhealthy beliefs and emotions you have absorbed throughout your life from your family, from traumatic experiences, and from your culture. IFS calls those beliefs and emotions your *burdens.* As your parts separate from the "you" that is left, you will begin experiencing and exhibiting those valuable leadership qualities (curiosity, compassion, and so on) and other ones because that is who you really are. As your parts trust that it is safe to separate from you, you will gradually experience more and more qualities of your Self. In that Self state, you will find that conversations with your parts go well and that you have an intuitive sense of how to listen to and then help them. Your therapist's primary job at this point is to help you stay in that Self state by noting when you shift out of it—catching different parts as they try to interfere and asking them to trust you and step back.

This process sounds pretty easy, and it happens smoothly when your parts have a great deal of trust in your Self. Many clients find, however, that when they ask parts to step back, their parts won't. You are likely to find this to be the case, too, at least initially or when dealing with particularly polarized parts. A part that won't step back often carries a great deal of responsibility for your welfare and fears that if it doesn't stick around, something dreadful will happen. Other parts fear that if they give up any control, they will be locked up or eliminated, or they are afraid that the part you want to work with will take over. There are many different reasons why parts are reluctant to give leadership to your Self. When they won't step back, your therapist will not try to force them to. Instead, he or she is likely to have you ask those parts why they are afraid to separate. Often they have good reasons—reasons that need to be addressed by your therapist until those parts feel satisfied that the feared consequence won't happen or can be handled in a safe manner.

In IFS, there is never a need to pressure or plead with parts to change. Instead, we try to listen to, reassure, and ask permission from them. We have great respect for the guardians of your inner world. They are trying their best to keep you safe, even if their attempts sometimes feel unnecessarily stifling or destructive. They have every right to keep the door shut to vulnerable territory within you, and we won't go into that territory without their permission. Sometimes your parts' fears are anachronistic. They may be stuck in the past when they needed to protect you in the way they do, and they don't know how much you and your situation have changed. Sometimes they just need an update about that. At other times, their fears are quite valid—perhaps concerns or consequences that you or your therapist didn't think of. For example, if you get closer to your anger, you might decide to leave your marriage, cut off from your father, or quit your job. And you might also get in touch with the grief that your anger protects and be overwhelmed by it. You and your therapist can discuss with your parts how valid each fear is and, if it seems to be a reasonable concern, how it will be addressed. Fortunately, after decades of exploring protective parts' fears, we have developed ways to handle the most common ones, such as being overwhelmed, for example. But there are often fears that are unique to your situation, and your therapist will collaborate with you to explore solutions. At times you and your therapist may agree that a protector's fear is valid and nothing can be done about it currently, so you decide to leave the door to an area of your inner work closed for the time being.

Thus, IFS work can be quite circuitous. You start out heading toward one part; get stuck, turn toward the part that is resisting, and work with it; and wind up in a totally different place than you expected. IFS therapists trust that your internal system has its own pace and wisdom about what needs to happen. We let your system unfold in its own time and only redirect when it feels as though a part is leading us on a wild goose chase or trying to distract. Even then, we simply ask the part to be direct about its fear rather than trying to protect in indirect ways. We also continually encourage you—your Self—to lead the way.

Sometimes when a client goes inside for the first time, it disturbs the protective parts more than they originally expected when they gave permission. When that's true, you may have thoughts telling you not to return to the therapist or, if you do return, not to let the therapist take you inside again. You might also have disturbing dreams or mysterious rushes of emotion during the week. This doesn't only happen the first time you go inside, but may occur several times during treatment as you continue the inward journey. Some of that is an expected, natural reaction whenever a person's inner ecology gets perturbed. It may also mean, however, that your therapist went too fast or too far. We ask that clients talk to their therapist about these reactions so they can be explored and assessed. IFS therapists should be highly sensitive to your feedback and adjust their approach accordingly. Also, let your therapist know if he or she doesn't seem fully present with you or if you sense a part of your therapist that bothers you. Your therapist knows he or she is encouraging you to enter delicate and sacred territory and wants you to trust that he or she is fully with you as you proceed. Your therapist welcomes your perceptions about that and will take them seriously; he or she will listen inside to see if any part is detected and will let you know the outcome of that search.

Thus, IFS is a collaborative process. Your Self and your therapist's Self set out together on a healing journey inside your system of parts. You are the expert on your experience—what you encounter on the journey—and he or she is an expert in helping you hold Self-leadership during the journey. At first, your therapist may direct things to some extent, but gradually you will have a natural tendency to take the lead, a tendency that your therapist will respect and encourage.

Returning once again to the example of anger, suppose that after some negotiating, the parts that guard your system have given permission to let you begin getting to know your anger. What will you want to know from it? If it's true that it's a good part stuck in a bad role (the "angry one"), it follows that you'd want to know what's keeping it in that role. If you ask a part a question like that from your heart, you are likely to hear about other parts that it is polarized with or is protecting. Your angry part may say it's afraid that if it doesn't stay angry, you'll get hurt. Following that line of questioning, you learn that your angry part stands in front of a vulnerable part that is easily hurt. So, on your journey so far, you meet first with protectors that try to keep everything in control in your life and are afraid of your anger. They give you permission to talk to an angry part that also turns out to be a protector of a vulnerable part. Next, your therapist is likely to have you ask the angry part for permission to work with the vulnerable one.

This is a common sequence in IFS work. We first help you get to know and appreciate the parts that protect your system. Because they are on guard all the time, they usually are not ready to be healed until your system is less vulnerable. So we ask permission to go to the vulnerable ones and heal them first. Once they are less vulnerable, your protectors relax a bit and will submit to the healing process. With many clients, that cycle—getting permission from protectors to heal vulnerable parts and then returning to protectors—is repeated many times because most people have many subgroupings of protector/vulnerable systems. The personality has often been compared to an onion with many layers surrounding an all-important core issue. IFS sees your personality more like a bulb of garlic with many different cloves (each one containing some protectors and one or two vulnerable parts), each of which needs to be worked with independently. As each one of those cloves changes, you are likely to experience a little more Self and a shift in the issue those parts revolved around—in this case, anger and vulnerability. Some people experience dramatic changes in themselves after a particular clove has been healed, but more often clients sense gradual increases in confidence, well-being, clarity, and calmness.

What do we mean by "healing a part"? What do parts need in order to heal? We have discovered over many years of doing IFS work that, generally, all that parts need to unburden—that is, to unload the extreme beliefs and emotions that keep them locked in rigid roles—is to believe that you fully understand what happened in the past when they acquired their burdens. In other words, they need you to compassionately witness a piece of your own history.

What is entailed in witnessing? After you've met and formed a trusting relationship with a vulnerable part, your therapist will say some version of the following: "Ask this part to show you what it wants you to know about the past." At that point, you may begin "seeing" scenes or images, as if you're watching a movie of yourself at a younger age. Or you may experience emotions or sensations without any visuals. The vulnerable part has begun to tell its story in the form that feels safest to it. Your therapist will have you stay focused on that story until the part believes you understand what happened and appreciate how bad it was.

After the part feels fully witnessed, your therapist will sometimes ask you to enter the scene and take the part (often you as a child) out of it. Sometimes, however, the step of retrieving a part from the past isn't needed.

Next, your therapist will have you ask the part if it's ready to unload the beliefs or emotions it took on from those painful experiences. It may seem hard to believe that unburdening could be this simple—that things that have plagued you your whole life could be lifted just by looking at where you got them. In many cases it is that simple, but just because it's simple doesn't mean it's easy. As we discussed earlier, you may have many reasons to fear revisiting certain events in your past or opening your heart to parts that are frozen in time during those events. Although the experience of witnessing is rarely as distressing as your protectors imagine it will be, it is often emotional and unpleasant. The good news is that it is usually over quickly, and most parts feel better immediately afterward. Once a vulnerable part has released its burden in this way, the parts that were protecting it or keeping it locked up often relax and become more interested in being healed themselves.

There are a few other steps involved in healing a part, but usually the witnessing is by far the hardest one, and it often takes many sessions before your protective parts will allow you to get there. Don't get frustrated if it takes awhile. It takes as long as it takes, and the part of you that wants to rush through the process ironically slows everything down because it makes other parts dig in their heels. If you have a pushing part like that, let your therapist know right away so the two of you can help it relax.

During the time when you are approaching a vulnerable part, you may experience an increase in impulsive behavior. For example, you may feel a strong urge to binge on food, alcohol, drugs, sex, or work. Or you may feel more suicidal or enraged. You might also notice an increase in physical symptoms, such as headaches, or other pains or illnesses. These are all common, predictable reactions of protective parts as you approach territory they are terrified to let you enter. Your therapist should take these reactions seriously by having you talk to the parts giving you those impulses or symptoms to see what kind of reassurance they need. Often all they need is for you and your therapist to go over again what you're doing, why, and whether your therapist might judge you or be otherwise untrustworthy. If, on the other hand, those impulsive parts need more structure to contain them, you and your therapist can brainstorm whatever alternatives might be necessary, including hospitalization or medication. But, often, all that's required is further reassurance and negotiation.

After a vulnerable part has unburdened, you might feel protective and not want to go inside again for awhile. You might also feel more distant from your therapist and even think about stopping treatment. You might be more prickly or withdrawn at home or at the office. It's good practice to warn those you live or work with that while you do this inner work, there will be times when you won't be yourself. All these are also predictable reactions to connecting with previously exiled vulnerable parts. Once a part has been healed, there's often a need to reorganize internally, and your protectors may be thrown off by that. If you can't find a cushion—a period of calm after such a session—you may find that the unburdening doesn't stick and you have to heal the part again. For this reason, clients often schedule sessions at times when they don't need to go back to work immediately and can be still for awhile.

Some clients don't remember everything that happened in sessions, so you may want to bring a tape recorder and listen to the tape during the week. Also, clients find that journaling helps them remember and stay with the process. They write about what happened during the session and what they do with or learn about their parts during the week. Some clients do a great deal of work with their parts between sessions, a process that speeds up the therapy. Others find that their parts only allow them to go inside in the presence of the therapist. That isn't a problem—it just causes the process to take a bit longer.

Again, every person's system is different—has different levels of fear, goes at a different pace, and has different quantities of burdens. Naturally, people with a great deal of abuse or trauma in their background take longer. Many people get discouraged at one time or another during the journey because it seems as if the number of parts they need to heal is endless. It may seem like that at times, but you can trust that you have a finite amount of pain to unburden and there will come a time when you'll feel much better. Another common discouraging experience comes after you have done a great deal of work and yet you react to something in the outside world in the same old way. You thought you were almost done, but it seems as though you're back to square one. Even though it seems that way, you aren't. Until you have healed all your vulnerable parts, you will have some protectors that will do their usual thing to protect. It's important for your therapist to help you keep perspective on how much has changed, even though some things haven't. The change process is often a roller coaster ride, and it helps to have a therapist who isn't on the roller coaster with you and who instead, to shift metaphors, can be the steady "I" in the storm for you.

There is no way to predict in advance how long your healing process will take, but you are free to decide at any time to change the frequency of meetings or to take a break. Your therapist will likely help you check to see what parts are involved in those kinds of decisions, but ultimately he or she will respect your choices.

There are also differences in how people experience the process. Some dread coming to therapy and often feel as if they are forcing themselves to continue—as if they're going to the dentist, but without the novocaine. Others are fascinated and invigorated by the whole process. If you're like most people, there will be times when you're fascinated and other times when you dread it. If your therapist can help you persist, you'll come out on the other side feeling proud of what you accomplished and glad about how much better you feel.

Appendix A: Overview of the IFS Model

I. **Parts**

    A. Subpersonalities, or aspects of our personality that interact internally in sequences and styles that are similar to the ways that people interact with each other.

    B. All parts are valuable and want to have a positive role. We are born with them or their potential; it is the nature of the mind to be subdivided. It is good to be multiple.

    C. Parts become extreme and can be destructive because of life experiences.

II. **Self**

    A. The seat of consciousness—a different level of entity than parts. Unlike parts, the Self is invisible because it is the "you" who is observing.

    B. The Self contains qualities such as compassion, confidence, curiosity, and perspective—qualities of good leadership. Everyone has such a Self, but it can be obscured by the extremes of parts.

III. **Basic Goals of the Model**

    A. To release parts from their extreme roles so they can find and adopt their preferred, valuable roles.

    B. To differentiate client's Self so the Self can help harmonize and balance his or her inner and outer life.

IV. **Assumptions**

A. As we develop, our parts form a complex system of interaction with polarizations and alliances. Systems theory and technology can be applied to the internal system. When the system reorganizes, parts can change rapidly.

B. Changes in the internal system will affect changes in the external system and vice versa. One can work with either to change the other.

V. **Three-Group Model of Common Parts Roles**

A. *Exiles:* Young, vulnerable parts that have experienced trauma and are isolated from the rest of the system for their own and the system's protection. Exiles carry the memories, sensations, and emotions of the events and are stuck in the past.

B. *Managers:* Parts that run the day-to-day life of the person. These parts try to keep exiles exiled by staying in control of events or relationships, being perfect and pleasing, caretaking, scaring the person out of taking risks by criticizing, apathy, worry, and so on.

C. *Firefighters:* Parts that react when exiles are activated in an effort to extinguish their feelings or dissociate the person from them. Common firefighter activities include: drug or alcohol use, self-mutilation (cutting), binge eating, sex binges, suicidal ideation, and rage. Firefighters have the same goals as managers (to keep exiles away) but different, more impulsive strategies.

VI. **Using the Model**

    A. Assess external system to make sure it is safe to do work.

    B. Introduce language; ask about relationship with different parts; ask about what the person would like to change.

    C. Work with managers first; discuss their fears and how they can be addressed; form collaborative relationship with them; respect their pace.

    D. Ask about and defuse any dangerous firefighters.

    E. With permission of managers, begin working with exiles. Do retrievals and unburdenings as appropriate.

    F. After each retrieval, ask how all parts are doing.

    G. Throughout, keep therapist parts from interfering, and welcome client feedback in parts detecting.

The Internal System

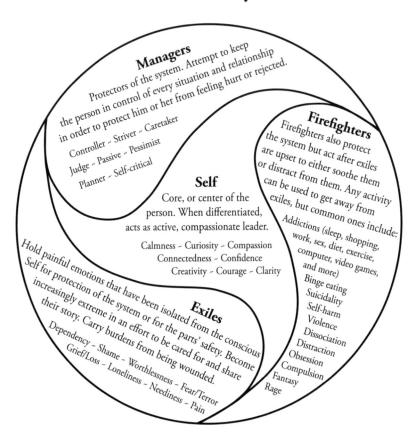

Managers
Protectors of the system. Attempt to keep the person in control of every situation and relationship in order to protect him or her from feeling hurt or rejected.

Controller ~ Striver ~ Caretaker
Judge ~ Passive ~ Pessimist
Planner ~ Self-critical

Firefighters
Firefighters also protect the system but act after exiles are upset to either soothe them or distract from them. Any activity can be used to get away from exiles, but common ones include:

Addictions (sleep, shopping, work, sex, diet, exercise, computer, video games, and more)
Binge eating
Suicidality
Self-harm
Violence
Dissociation
Distraction
Obsession
Compulsion
Fantasy
Rage

Self
Core, or center of the person. When differentiated, acts as active, compassionate leader.

Calmness ~ Curiosity ~ Compassion
Connectedness ~ Confidence
Creativity ~ Courage ~ Clarity

Exiles
Hold painful emotions that have been isolated from the conscious Self for protection of the system or for the parts' safety. Become increasingly extreme in an effort to be cared for and share their story. Carry burdens from being wounded.

Dependency ~ Shame ~ Worthlessness ~ Fear/Terror
Grief/Loss ~ Loneliness ~ Neediness ~ Pain

Text adapted from *Internal Family Systems Therapy* by Richard C. Schwartz, Ph.D.
Graphic by Janet R. Mullen, LCSW

Appendix B: IFS Glossary

Balance
A state in which members of a human system have equitable access to the responsibilities, resources, and influence they need.

Blending
When the feelings and beliefs of one part merge with another part or the Self.

Burdens
Extreme ideas or feelings that are carried by parts and govern their lives. Burdens are left on or in parts from exposure to an external person or event.

Constraining Environment
A human systems environment characterized by imbalance, polarization, enmeshment, and problematic leadership. Constraining environments impose burdens on the systems within them.

Enmeshment
A state in which two members (or two groups) in a system become highly interdependent to the point where both parties' access to their Selves is constrained because their parts are so reactive to one another.

Exiles
Parts that have been sequestered within a system for their own protection or for the protection of the system from them.

Firefighters
Parts that go into action after the exiles have been activated in order to calm the exiles or distract the system from them (dissociation).

Harmony
A state in which the members of a human system relate collaboratively, with effective communication, mutual caring, and a sense of connection.

Imbalance
A state in which one member (or a group) has more or less access to responsibilities, influence, and resources.

Managers   Parts that try to run a system in ways that minimize the activation of exiles.

Multiplicity   The recognition that the human mind is not
Paradigm   unitary but instead is naturally subdivided into a multitude of subpersonalities.

Parts   The term used in Internal Family Systems for a person's subpersonalities. Parts are best considered internal people of different ages, talents, and temperaments.

Polarization   A state in which two members (or two groups) in a system relate in opposition to or in competition with each other, to the point where each party's access to the Self is constrained by fear that the other party will win or take over.

Problematic   A state in which leaders of a system have
Leadership   abdicated, are biased, are polarized with each other or have been discredited.

Self   The core of a person, which contains leadership qualities such as compassion, perspective, curiosity, and confidence. The Self is best equipped to lead the internal family.

Self-Leadership   Leadership characterized by compassion, calmness, clarity, curiosity, confidence, courage, creativity, and connectedness.

Sustaining   A human systems environment characterized
Environment   by balance, harmony, and effective leadership.

Appendix C: Selected IFS Readings

Breunlin, D., Schwartz, R., and Karrer, B. (1992). *Metaframeworks: Transcending the models of family therapy.* San Francisco: Jossey Bass.

Goulding, R. and Schwartz, R. (2002). *The mosaic mind: Empowering the tormented selves of child abuse survivors.* Trailheads Publications, Oak Park, IL.

Nichols, M. and Schwartz, R. (2004). *Family therapy concepts and methods.* 6th Edition. New York: Allyn & Bacon.

Schwartz, R. (1987). Our multiple selves. *Family Therapy Networker, 11,* 24–31.

Schwartz, R. (1988). Know they selves. *Family Therapy Networker, 12,* 21–29.

Schwartz, R. (1992). Rescuing the exiles. *Family Therapy Networker,* May-June, pp. 33–37, 75.

Schwartz, R. (1995). *Internal Family Systems Therapy.* New York: Guilford.

Schwartz, R. (2001). *Introduction to the Internal Family Systems Model.* Oak Park, IL: Trailheads Publications.

Schwartz, R. (2008). *You are the one you've been waiting for: Bringing courageous love to intimate relationships.* Oak Park, IL: Trailheads Publications.

References

Abramsky, S. (1999). When they get out. *Atlantic Monthly, 283* (6), pp. 30–36.

Allison, R. B. (1974). A new treatment approach for multiple personality disorder. *American Journal of Clinical Hypnosis, 17,* pp. 15–32.

Allison, R. B. & Schwartz, T. (1980). *Minds in many pieces.* New York: Rawson-Wade.

Armstrong, K. (1993). *A history of God.* New York: Ballantine.

Bawa Muhaiyaddeen, M. R. (1994). The holy war within. In R. Fields (Ed.), *The Awakened Warrior.* New York: Jeremy Tarcher.

Bianco, Margery Williams (1999). *The velveteen rabbit.* New York: HarperCollins.

Boorstein, S. (1980). *Transpersonal psychotherapy.* Palo Alto: Science and Behavior Books.

Borysenko, J. (1999). *A woman's journey to God.* New York: Riverhead Books.

Capra, F. (1996). *The web of life.* New York: Anchor Books.

Carney, J. (1997). *Unique advances and psychospiritual contributions of internal family systems therapy in clinical work with gay men, lesbians, ambisexuals, and their families.* Unpublished manuscript.

Childre, D. & Martin, H. (1999). *The Heartmath solution.* San Francisco: HarperSanFrancisco.

Chodron, P. (1994). *Start where you are.* Boston: Shambhala Press.

Chodron, P. (1998). A practice of compassion. In H. Palmer (Ed.), *Inner knowing.* New York: Jeremy Tarcher.

Close, E. (2000). The prison paradox. *Newsweek,* Nov. 13, pp. 42–49.

Comstock, C. (1991). The inner self helper and concepts of inner guidance. *Dissociation, 4* (3), pp. 165–175.

Coon, D. (1992). Testing the limits of sense and science. *American Psychologist, 47* (2), pp. 143–151.

Csikszentmihalyi, M. (1990). *Flow.* New York: Harper & Row.

Deikman, A. (1982). *The observing self.* Boston: Beacon Press.

Dillard, A. (1999). *For the time being.* New York: Knopf.

Edwards, B. (1986). *Drawing on the right side of the brain.* New York: Simon & Schuster.

Ehrenreich, B. (1999). Nickel-and-dimed: on (not) getting by in America. *Harpers,* Jan., pp. 37–52.

Faludi, S. (1999). Rage of the American male. *Newsweek,* Aug 16, p. 31.

Ford, D. (1998). *The dark side of the light chasers.* New York: Riverhead Books.

Gallwey, T. (1979). *The inner game of tennis.* New York: Bantam Books.

Goleman, D. (1995). *Emotional intelligence.* New York: Bantam Books.

Gould, S. J. (1997). A tale of two worksites. *Natural History, 106,* pp. 18–22, 29, 62–68.

Green, A. (1977). *Your world is on fire.* New York: Schocken Books.

Green, E. & Green, A. (1977). *Beyond biofeedback.* Fort Wayne, IN: Knoll Publishing.

Grigg, R. (1994). *The tao of Zen.* Edison, NJ: Alva Press.

Hadot, P. (1993). *Plotinus.* Chicago: University of Chicago Press.

Hammen, D. & Peters, D. (1978). Interpersonal consequences of depression: responses of men and women enacting a depressed role. *Journal of Abnormal Psychology, 87,* pp. 322–32.

Hammer, M. (1999). *Is work bad for you? Atlantic Monthly, 284* (2), pp. 87–93.

Harner, M. (1996). Shamanic healing: we are not alone. *Alternative Therapies, 2* (3), pp. 69–75.

Huxley, A. (1944). *The perennial philosophy.* New York: Harper & Row.

Ingerman, S. (1991). *Soul retrieval: Mending the fragmented self.* San Francisco: HarperSanFrancisco.

Jaworski, J. (1996). *Synchronicity: The inner path of leadership.* San Francisco: Berrett-Koehler Publishers.

Jung, C. G. (1962). *Memories, dreams, reflections* (Rev. Ed.). Aniela Jaffe (Ed.). New York: Pantheon Books.

Keating, T. (1998). *Open heart/open mind.* New York: Continuum.

Keating, T. (1999). *The human condition.* Mahwah, NJ: Paulist Press.

Keen, S. (1994a). *Hymns to an unknown god.* New York: Bantam.

Keen, S. (1994b). The virtue of moral outrage. In R. Fields (Ed.), *The awakened warrior.* New York: Jeremy Tarcher.

King, M. L. (1994). Pilgrimage to nonviolence. In R. Fields (Ed.), *The awakened warrior.* New York: Jeremy Tarcher.

Kohn, A. (1986). *No contest: The case against competition.* New York: Houghton Mifflin.

Kornfield, J. (1993). *A path with heart.* New York: Bantam.

Kraft, K. (Ed.) (1988). *Zen: Tradition and transition.* New York: Grove Press.

Lama, D. & Cutler, H. (1998). *The art of happiness.* New York: Riverhead Books.

Lamott, A. (1994). *Bird by bird.* New York: Anchor Books.

Lamott, A. (1999). *Traveling mercies.* New York: Pantheon Books.

LePage, V. (1999). The god debate. *Quest, 87* (6), pp. 212–215.

Levoy, G. (1997). *Callings: Finding and following an authentic life.* New York: Three Rivers Press.

McConnell, S. (1999). Our bodies? Our selves? *Self to Self: Newsletter of the IFSA, 4* (3), pp. 1–5.

Merton, T. (1965). *The way of Chuang Tzu.* New York: New Directions.

Metzger, D. (1992). Personal disarmament. In J. Welwood, (Ed.), *Ordinary magic: Everyday life as a spiritual path.* Boston: Shambhala Press.

Metzner, R. (1994). Getting to know one's inner enemies. In R. Fields (Ed.), *The awakened warrior.* New York: Jeremy Tarcher.

Miller, A. (1994). *The drama of the gifted child: The search for the true self.* New York: Basic Books.

Miller, D. (1974). *The new polytheism.* New York: Harper & Row.

Mitchell, S. (Ed.) (1991). *The enlightened mind: An anthology of sacred prose.* New York: HarperCollins.

Munsterburg, H. (1910). *American problems from the point of view of a psychologist.* New York: Moffat, Yard.

Muwakkil, D. (2000). Voters clearly punched 'no' to war on drugs. *Chicago Tribune,* Nov. 20, p. 15.

Newton, M. (1999). *Journey of souls.* St. Paul, MN: Llewellyn Publications.

Nhat Hanh, T. (1992). *Peace is every step.* New York: Bantam Books.

Pagels, E. (1979). *The Gnostic gospels.* New York: Vintage Books.

Pagels, E. (1995). *The origin of Satan.* New York: Vintage Books.

Pennebaker, J. (1997). *Opening up: The healing power of expressing emotions.* New York: Guilford Publications.

Pennington, M. B. (1993). *Thomas Merton: My brother.* New York: New City Press.

Po-Tuan, C. (1986). *The inner teachings of Taoism* (T. Cleary, Trans.). Boston: Shambhala Press. (Original work written in eleventh century)

Real, T. (1997). *I don't want to talk about it: Overcoming the secret legacy of male depression.* New York: Fireside.

Reed, H. (1989). *Edgar Cayce: On channeling the higher self.* New York: Warner Books.

Rilke, R. M. (1984). *Letters to a young poet* (S. Mitchell, Trans.). New York: Vintage Books. (Original work published 1903)

Schwartz, T. (1995). *What really matters.* New York: Bantam.

Shumsky, D. (1996). *Divine revelation.* New York: Simon & Shuster.

Siegel, D. (1999). *The developing mind.* New York: Guilford Publications.

Smith, H. (1989). *Beyond the post-modern mind.* Wheaton, IL: The Theosophical Publishing House.

Smith, M. (1997). *Jung and shamanism in dialogue.* New York: Paulist Press.

Smoley, R. & Kinne, J. (1999). *Hidden wisdom: A guide to the Western inner traditions.* New York: The Penguin Group.

Sullivan, A. (2000). The he hormone. *New York Times Magazine.* April 2, pp. 46–51.

Walker, A. (1998). *By the light of my father's smile.* New York: Ballantine Books.

Watzlawick, P., Weakland, J., & Fisch, R. (1974). *Change.* New York: Jason Aronson.

Wegner, D. (1994). *White bears and other unwanted thoughts.* New York: Guilford Publications.

Welwood, J. (1996). *Love and awakening.* New York: HarperCollins.

Wilber, K. (1977). *The spectrum of consciousness.* Wheaton, IL: Quest.

Wilber, K. (1985). *No boundary.* Boston: Shambhala Press.

Wilber, K. (1995). *Sex, ecology, spirituality.* Boston: Shambhala Press.

Wilber, K. (1996). *A brief history of everything.* Boston: Shambhala Press.

Wilber, K. (1997). *The eye of spirit.* Boston: Shambhala Press.

Wypijewski, J. (1999). A boy's life. *Harpers.* September, vol. 299.

Internal
Family
Systems℠

For more information
about IFS trainings and therapy,
contact:

The Center for Self Leadership
P.O. Box 3969
Oak Park, IL 60303
Telephone: 708.383.2659
Fax: 708.383.2399
INFO@selfleadership.org
www.selfleadership.org